# Praying In The Presence Of

# Our Lord

## WITH
## DOROTHY
## DAY

To Donna
with Love
&
Thanks
the Renew
Core

# Praying In The Presence Of
# Our Lord

## WITH
## DOROTHY
## DAY

# DAVID SCOTT

### FR. BENEDICT J. GROESCHEL, C.F.R.
#### SERIES EDITOR

Our Sunday Visitor Publishing Division
Our Sunday Visitor, Inc.
Huntington, Indiana 46750

*Nihil Obstat:*
Rev. Michael Heintz
Censor Librorum

*Imprimatur:*
✠ John M. D'Arcy
Bishop of Fort Wayne-South Bend
June 23, 2002

The *Nihil Obstat* and *Imprimatur* are declarations that a work is free
from doctrinal or moral error. It is not implied that those who have
granted the *Nihil Obstat* and *Imprimatur* agree with the contents,
opinions, or statements expressed.

Scripture citations, contained in the writings of Dorothy Day, are from
a number of editions, which she did not identify. Quotations from her
works have been transcribed verbatim, except for italicizing the
Scripture citations she uses and some stylistic changes for consistency.
Every reasonable effort has been made to determine copyright holders
and to secure permissions as needed. If any copyrighted materials have
been inadvertently used in this work without proper credit being given
in one manner or another, please notify Our Sunday Visitor in writing
so that future editions may be corrected accordingly.

ISBN: 0-87973-909-6 (Inventory No. 909)
LCCN: 2002107144

Cover design by Tyler Ottinger
Cover art by Robert F. McGovern
Interior design by Sherri L. Hoffman

PRINTED IN THE UNITED STATES OF AMERICA

✠
_____

*For Louise and Mark Zwick,*
*Tom Cornell and Michael Garvey,*
*Fred Boehrer and Diana Conroy*

# Table of Contents

✠

# Preface

✠

*I*f you have used any of the short volumes in this series of books for Eucharistic adoration, you may be surprised to see that we are now including that old Catholic anarchist, Dorothy Day, placing her in the company of St. Thomas Aquinas and Bishop Sheen. Older Catholics knew Dorothy Day generally as a devout gadfly, admired for her love and work for the poor, but also as something of an eccentric and holy crank. Younger Catholics, unless they are readers of the *Catholic Worker* or of her autobiographical account, *The Long Loneliness*, or unless they are specifically involved in Christian social action, will know little about Dorothy and may not even be able to call to mind the social climate and times in which her witness was so important to the Church.

Even to her contemporaries, Dorothy was an enigma. Having had the privilege of knowing Dorothy, I recall her as a person of disconcerting surprises. When I first went to visit the Catholic Worker movement and meet this radical Catholic, I was completely mystified to see on her desk a large framed photograph of Cardinal McIntyre of Los Angeles attired in miter and cope. The photo was inscribed "To my dear friend Dorothy Day." When I came to know her better, I was once confronted by Dorothy in her denunciation mode, waving her fist at me while clutching an old black Rosary. A priest had performed a marriage of a divorced person without an annulment, and somehow Dorothy heard that I had performed the ceremony. I recall the lioness of Judah backing off when she realized she had the wrong clerical culprit.

Dorothy was a radical in the true sense of the word, which derives from the Latin *radix*, or root. She always went to the root of things. Words like "liberal" or "conservative" did not fit Dorothy. If any contemporary term fits her, it is "dynamically orthodox" or "completely committed." And in every sense of the word, she was devout.

Dorothy can be best understood when we fit her into the historical framework of the great women reformers of the Church: Sts. Catherine of Siena, Catherine of Genoa, and Teresa of Ávila; Catherine Doherty (Baroness de Hueck), Mother Teresa of Calcutta, and even Mother Angelica. All these people have had armies of critics and enemies. Unlike almost all men, even men reformers, these valiant women were absolutists. As the saying goes, "They took no prisoners." If we read the selections here prayerfully in the Eucharistic presence, we will come away quite aware that we need to change or redefine our ideas about the poor, the rich, the world, our neighbors, the sacraments, and the priesthood — even Our Lord and the kingdom of God. We will begin to think in absolutes.

This fine book will reveal the thoughts and prayers of a soul drawn irresistibly to the poor suffering Christ. Since the days of the Church Fathers, like Sts. Augustine and John Chrysostom, and especially since Sts. Bernard, Dominic, and Francis, the vision of Christ in the suffering and the poor has been linked with the holy Eucharist. Those who criticize Eucharistic devotion as separated from our realistic responsibilities to others should be completely silenced by this book. On the other hand, those who are already dedicated to prayerful Eucharistic devotion will learn from Dorothy Day that you cannot adore Christ in the Blessed Sacrament and walk past Him begging in the street or suffering among the shut-ins.

Although I did not know Dorothy as well as I knew Mother Teresa, firsthand observation of each of these remarkable women made it crystal clear that the love of Christ in the Eucharist and His love for the poor and needy were not only linked but for them were really inseparable phases of the same reality.

Her touching devotion to the priesthood, and especially to the loving and unworldly priests she mentions, is a powerful object lesson for both laity and clergy in these times of clerical scandal. She loved poor and dedicated priests, but she had friends and admirers who were cardinals. At the time of her death, in fact, Cardinal Cooke stated his opinion that she was a saint. Cardinal O'Connor began the first stages of examining a possible cause of beatification.

Most of all, Dorothy Day can lead us to a far more enticing and awesome devotion to Jesus Christ. David Scott has combed her works and found treasures. Dorothy will never leave you bored. Her love for the suffering Christ is as haunting today as it was years ago when the startling engravings of Fritz Eichenberg brought the face of the humble Christ to the front page of the *Catholic Worker*. One of her favorite quotations must be pondered while looking at a crucifix. These words of Dostoyevsky, spoken by the saintly Father Zossima in *The Brothers Karamazov*, sum up Dorothy's pilgrimage: "Love in practice is a harsh and dreadful thing compared to love in dreams."

Take this book with you before the Blessed Sacrament. It may not always lead you to the most peaceful meditation, but if you pray fervently and truly in Christ's presence, you will be changed. You will come closer to Christ as He really is. That is, after all, the most you can expect any book to do.

*Father Benedict J. Groeschel, C.F.R.*

# Thanks

☩

To my mom and dad, Carole and Brian Scott, for the gift of faith and for supporting all my research and writing in more ways than just financially. To my wife, Sarah, for everything, not only for spending many cold winter evenings in the basement of the Duquesne University Library helping me photocopy every word Dorothy Day ever wrote from crumbling editions of *The Catholic Worker.* To my children: Hannah, Brigid, Cecilia, Jacob, and Charles, who make everything worthwhile. To Msgr. Rich Antall, Mike Aquilina, David Easter, and Greg Erlandson for their friendship and encouragement every step of the way. To Dorothy Day and Father John Hugo and the Blessed Mother for their prayers.

# Introduction

✠

$D$orothy Day's story seems straight out of one of those capsule lives-of-the-saints she used to read every day in her old *St. Andrew Missal.*

Born in Brooklyn on November 8, 1897, she was a lonely, bookish kid who grew up on the lower side of middle class, the third of five children. As a child, she bounced across the country to California as her father, a journeyman sportswriter, chased work. She was there when the great San Francisco earthquake hit, and some of her first apprehensions of God are tangled up in nightmares of dishes rattling in cupboards and dark rumblings beneath the floorboards.

The Days finally settled in Chicago, taking a flat above a saloon. Even in her late seventies, Dorothy could evoke the "interminable gray streets, fascinating in their sameness . . . tavern after tavern . . . block after block." She recalled the frayed lives, the smells of garbage and stale beer, the hideous laugh of a neighbor lady roasting a rat she had trapped, the frightened eyes of a bloodied "scab" who took refuge in their apartment after being beaten by striking unionists.

Though her parents were not church-goers, from an early age Dorothy said she always felt "haunted by God." She was baptized Episcopalian at twelve and by then was reading the New Testament and the Psalms, *The Imitation of Christ*, and the legends of the martyrs. She would fast and sleep on hardwood floors to mortify her flesh and she wrote breathlessly in her little red diary about wanting to suffer for the sins of the world.

When her fall came, Dorothy went down hard. Reading *The Jungle*, Upton Sinclair's savage exposé of Chicago's meat-packing industry, drew her out of pious introspection and plunged her into the rising radical tide of 1910s America. It was an era of unrest and expectancy that we can scarce imagine today — when trade unions like the Industrial Workers of the World were drawing up blueprints for a nationwide strike that would drive the capitalist system to its knees, when Socialist Party candidate Eugene Debs could poll close to a million votes in his bid for the presidency.

Dorothy dropped out of college and headed to New York, taking a job as a reporter for the country's largest socialist daily, *The Call*. She chronicled the desperate straits of the urban "proletariat" in grim dispatches with tabloid headlines like "Mr. J. D. Rockefeller, 26 Broadway, Here's a Family Living on Dog Food" — writing to stir the ire of the poor, to incite the inevitable class war.

Revolution was in the air, and for much of the next decade Dorothy Day breathed deep. She threw herself into the progressive causes of the moment — working for the Anti-Conscription League, shilling a little for Margaret Sanger's birth-control crusade, writing propaganda for anti-imperialists helping Sandino's guerrillas in Nicaragua. She was arrested outside the White House protesting for women's right to vote, and wound up spending thirty days in prison in solitary confinement.

Dorothy cast her lot, too, with the crowd of bohemian artists and actors, free-thinkers, free-lovers, and lowlifes who haunted the experimental playhouses and whiskey bars of Greenwich Village. Many a night was spent in the smoky backrooms of dive saloons with names like *The Hell Hole*, romancing and idling with the likes of the playwright Eugene O'Neill. Stories of her ability to drink longshoremen under the table became part of Village literary lore.

What Dorothy called her "flaming youth" ended with her becoming one of many tragic casualties in the other revolution going on at the time — the sexual revolution. She was forced into an abortion by one lover, who had threatened to leave her if she kept the baby and then left her anyway. She married on the rebound to a wealthy literary agent, and they lived for a year in Paris and Italy before breaking up.

Dorothy drifted back to Chicago, wrote for some left-wing publications, and was thrown into jail in one of the federal government's anti-communist "Red raids." She went down to New Orleans with her sister, worked for a while on a muckraking commercial newspaper, going undercover to write a series on drugs and vice in the city's dance-halls.

In 1924, she published a painfully transparent auto-biographical novel, *The Eleventh Virgin*. "Just one more adolescent novel," was how *The New York Times* reviewer dismissed it. Nonetheless, Dorothy was able to sell the movie rights for five thousand dollars (the movie was never produced). She used the money to buy a bungalow in a left-wing artists' colony back in Staten Island, New York.

There she fell in love and entered into a common-law marriage with an anarchist nature-lover, Forster

Batterham. And in the tranquil beauty and simplicity of life on the beach with the man she loved, Dorothy Day started to pray again, clutching a Rosary a friend had given her years ago.

She had long since abandoned the pieties of her adolescence, and she believed ardently with her radical friends that religion was "the opiate of the masses," a false promise of "pie in the sky when you die." But in times of distress and uncertainty she had always turned back to the Bible, especially to the Psalms. And wherever she lived, she was known to end a long night of drinking and carousing by ducking into a neighborhood Catholic church, to sit alone in the damp darkness, watching the votive candles flicker and glow.

On that beach — fishing in the bay, walking barefoot along the shore, gathering horseshoe crabs, shells, and mussels, the sun and salt on her face, the wind in her hair —Dorothy confronted the reality that such a beautiful creation must have a Creator. The crowning beauty of that creation, for her the greatest possible gift of the Creator, would be the child she bore to Forster in the early spring of 1927. As she would later write: "Such a great feeling of happiness and joy filled me that I was hungry for Someone to thank, to love, even to worship, for so great a good that had been bestowed upon me."

The baby she named Tamar, and she had her baptized Catholic. "I was not going to have her floundering through many years as I had done, doubting and hesitating, undisciplined and amoral," she explained. But she knew the decision would cost her her mate.

Forster, an atheist, had found it impossible to relate to Dorothy's emerging faith in those months on the beach.

He threw up a stony wall of silence at her every mention of religion or God. By the time he walked out for good later that year, Dorothy had decided to be baptized herself. She was received into the Catholic Church on December 28, 1927, and confirmed the following year at Pentecost.

A single mother now, and a Catholic, she moved back to New York City to work. She did a stint with Metro-Goldwyn-Mayer, evaluating new novels for possible film adaptations. She and Tamar went out to Hollywood where she wrote dialogue for another film studio. She wrote for Catholic periodicals like *Commonweal* and *America*.

All the time she felt pangs of guilt and betrayal, as if her conversion had fixed an impassable gulf between her and the poor and working classes. In moments of weakness, she wondered whether in becoming Catholic she had sold out the poor, abandoned the cause of justice and social change, gone over to the enemy. Her anxious search for direction came to a head in December 1932, while covering a communist-led "hunger march of the unemployed" in Washington, D.C.

Watching the bedraggled men file by, she experienced an epiphany of sorts: "These are Christ's poor. He was one of them. . . . These men feel they have been betrayed by Christianity. . . . Far dearer in the sight of God perhaps are these hungry ragged ones, than all those smug, well-fed Christians who sit in their homes, cowering in fear of the communist menace."

The next day was the day Catholics celebrate the Virgin Mary's "Immaculate Conception." Dorothy went to the high Mass at the shrine in the nation's capitol and prayed a desperate prayer to the Virgin — "that some way would be opened up for me to work for the poor and the oppressed." She came home to find a vagabond French peasant-intellectual, Peter Maurin, camped out on her doorstep looking for somebody to help him propagate what he called a "green revolution."

Together on May 1, 1933, they launched something they called "the Catholic Worker" in New York's Lower East Side. The movement's ambition was nothing short of starting a revolution — calling the alienated workers of the world to unite around Christ and the Catholic Church's vision for a new world order.

They started a shelter and soup kitchen to provide "Christian hospitality" to the unemployed and homeless. They started a commune in the countryside to put into practice Maurin's ideas of "cult, culture, and cultivation" — small, self-sustaining communities of work and worship based on farming, simple industry, and handicrafts.

They started a newspaper to spread their ideas for building "a new society within the shell of the old." And the movement grew, with new houses of hospitality and farming communes cropping up across the country, each with unique concerns and personalities, each drawing inspiration and encouragement from the vision articulated month to month by Dorothy Day in the pages of *The Catholic Worker.*

It was a radical Catholic vision of the world as God intended it to be, and Dorothy wrote with a prophet's indignation at what men and women in their sinfulness had made of this world. She opposed with equal vehemence communism and capitalism, convicting both of robbing people of their dignity as persons created in the image and likeness of God.

Her critique of the American welfare state and consumer society was withering. Entertainment media, advertising, banks, the credit and finance industry, big business, and the military-industrial complex — all formed a "filthy, rotten system," organized and operating for the benefit of the few at the expense of the many, she said.

Dorothy spoke out, too, on the wars of her day. She decried the persecutions in Mexico and Spain, opposed the Nazis, cried out against the holocaust of the Jews, the gulags of the Soviets, neo-colonial struggles from Latin America to Africa. Yet from the "Good War" to the Cold War to Vietnam, she remained absolute in her pacifist convictions. "If Our Lord were alive today, He would say as He said to St. Peter, 'Put up thy sword,' " she said.

Dorothy believed in the literal force of Christ's commandments to love the enemy and turn the other cheek. She took Him at His word, too, that in the end we will be judged by our love for Him as He comes to us in the poor and the prisoner, the sick and the stranger.

But her writing was so much more than politics and principles, issues and answers. She was probably the finest American diarist of her times. Like the novelists she loved, Dickens and Dostoyevsky, she could evoke mood and sense of place using clear, sensual images that were immediate and alive, that made you smell the smells, hear the sounds, and see the faces she wrote about.

Her columns in *The Catholic Worker* were long, winding affairs, ruminating on the issues of the day, the books she was reading, an opera she had just heard on the radio, the prayers said at Mass, the way the light slanted through the tree outside her window, chitchat from the house, a story from the lives of the saints, her daily struggles to make ends meet, to keep the faith.

She wrote as she lived, with a natural, unaffected sense of the "sacramental." She seemed genuinely able to live every day as if on pilgrimage, as if each moment could be a sacrament, a disclosure of the divine, a real encounter with the living God. She could sense the hidden presence of Jesus in the bread and wine at the altar, and in the poor and the hungry she served. She could abandon herself to the loving Providence of God, which she could see at work everywhere in the quiet mysteries of daily living.

Dorothy believed that every Catholic, nourished by the Eucharist and by prayer and the devotions of the Church, could live with this kind of attitude, indeed should be at the vanguard of bringing this sacramental vision to a world in the thrall of blind ideologies, war, and greed. This was "the revolution of the heart" that she preached. "There is nothing so radical, or so subversive, as Christianity," she wrote.

As radical as she was, Dorothy felt no hesitancy, no contradiction, in describing herself as a devout and obedient daughter of "Holy Mother Church." On occasion, she would even refer to the Pope as "Our dear, sweet Christ on earth," as St. Catherine of Siena used to call him in the thirteenth century. For Dorothy, the Catholic Church continued on earth the divine, saving presence of Jesus.

And she loved the Church with the thankfulness and joy of one whose life had been spared though she did not deserve it, as one who had experienced the saving love and mercy of God, as one who would remain eternally grateful for the gift of faith. Five years before her death, she wrote: "As Zechariah sang out, *We have knowledge of salvation through forgiveness of our sins.* I don't think anyone recognizes the comfort of this text better than I do."

Dorothy opposed every effort to dilute or undermine the Church's witness to the gospel of Jesus, every failure of Church leaders and ordinary Catholics to live up to the tremendous ideals and the teachings Jesus entrusted to His Church. She condemned the scandal of princes of the Church sprinkling holy water on bomber planes, of Catholic industrialists mistreating their workers, of "business-like priests" ignoring injustice and the plight of the poor.

When a new generation of Catholic radicals came along in the 1960s, declaring Church teachings on sexual morality to be obsolete and irrelevant, she gave them, too, a dressing down: "Birth control and abortion are genocide. . . . Make room for children, don't do away with them," she said.

Dorothy Day died on November 29, 1980, and was laid to rest in a simple casket in a donated grave not far from the bungalow on Staten Island where she first turned to God. She may have been one of the most visible and intriguing witnesses to Christ that America has ever produced — a single, working grandmother living in the slums, who prayed the Rosary and went to Mass every day, who marched on picket lines with longshoremen in the 1930s and farmworkers in the 1970s, who went to jail protesting war games and took Communion from the hands of the Pope.

For nearly fifty years, she lived without a salary among the poorest of the poor, supported solely by the prayers and donations of friends and sympathizers. By the end of her life she had brought her message of holy poverty and the works of mercy personally to the poor in nearly every state in America and in Rome and Russia, Africa, Cuba, Mexico, and India. And her influence on the Church continues today, not only in the one hundred eighty-five Catholic Worker communities in the United States and around the world, but in new generations of clergy and lay people attracted by her holiness and witness to love.

But what was Dorothy Day really like? The late J. Edgar Hoover, who had his Federal Bureau of Investigation spying on her for decades, thought he knew. Three times he tried to bring her up on charges of sedition, but the U.S. Attorney General refused. In the five-hundred-page FBI dossier he compiled on her, Hoover includes this less-than-flattering personal opinion: "Dorothy Day has been described as a very erratic and irresponsible person. . . . She maintains a very hostile and belligerent attitude towards the Bureau and makes every effort to castigate the Bureau whenever she feels so inclined."

True enough, Dorothy was no fan of government spooks. But probably a better picture of her was that offered by critic and political commentator Dwight Macdonald. His long 1952 profile in *The New Yorker* magazine reads like a bemused memo from a sympathetic yet unconverted bystander:

Many people think that Dorothy Day is a saint and that she will someday be canonized. . . . In her sensible shoes and her drab, well-worn clothes, Miss Day looks like an elderly school-teacher or librarian; she has the typical air of mild authority and of being no longer surprised at anything children or book-borrowers may do. She also looks like a grandmother, which she is, for her daughter now has five children.

Upon first meeting her, most people who are familiar with her career are surprised to find that, far from being dynamic, she is quiet and almost diffident. Although she has been speaking in public for years, her platform manner is retiring and hesitant, and she makes not even a stab at rhetorical effect. She has no "presence" at all, but in spite of that, or perhaps because of it, she is impressive to meet or to hear, communicating a moral force compounded of openness, sincerity, earnestness, and deprecatory humor. . . .

She is more a feeler and a doer than a thinker. Her mind works by free association rather than logic and her writing and public talks — "speeches" would hardly be the right word — are as haphazardly put together as her clothes. Her temperament combines mystical feeling and practicality in a way not common in the every-day world but not uncommon in the annals of hagiography.

Whether Dorothy Day winds up enrolled in the annals of hagiography is now for authorities in Rome to decide. On February 7, 2000, the late Cardinal John J. O'Connor of New York asked the Vatican to begin the usually long and painstaking investigative process needed to determine whether Dorothy Day should be canonized as an official "saint" of the Roman Catholic Church.

Cardinal O'Connor left no doubt where he stood on the matter: "It has long been my contention that Dorothy Day is a saint — not a 'gingerbread' saint or a 'holy card' saint, but a modern-day devoted daughter of the Church." In his petition to the Vatican, the cardinal compared her conversion story to that of the Church's most famous sinner-turned-saint, St. Augustine, and suggested her life could show to women who have had abortions "the mercy of God — mercy in that a woman who sinned so gravely could find such unity with God upon conversion."

He noted that her writings "are in complete fidelity to the Church" and that her thoughts on social-justice issues, so radical and controversial in her day, "anticipated the teachings of Pope John Paul II." And, the cardinal said, in "her complete commitment to pacifism in imitation of Christ," she was "like so many saints of days gone by" calling men and women "to live on earth the life they would one day lead in heaven, a life of peace and harmony."

Dorothy's mentor, the saintly Peter Maurin, used to say we should read history through the lives of the saints. In his view, the saints functioned as something like God's chorus, commenting by their lives and witness on the drama unfolding on the stage of human history at any given time or place.

If this is true, then there is much that God was trying to tell us about our times through the life of Dorothy Day — about the dignity of the human person, about the meaning of freedom and truth, about the relation of the Christian to the state, of the individual Catholic to the Church, about war and peace, rich and poor, about how to live a holy life in unholy times.

Dorothy called it "the way of love," the way of doing all for Jesus. She used to quote the great Jesuit theologian Henri de Lubac, who said: "When we choose the poor, we can always be sure of not going wrong. . . . We have chosen like Jesus. And we have chosen Jesus."

That is what she did. Dorothy chose the poor. Chose like Jesus. Chose Jesus. In so doing, she found herself on a secret path, a path that took her among the left-alone and the uncared-for, among those thought by the world to be no one and nothing. There, on what she called "the downward path that leads to salvation," she found unexpected beauties, unrepeatable love. There she found Jesus.

As she wrote in her memoir, *From Union Square to Rome:* "Sometimes in thinking and wondering at God's goodness to me, I have thought that . . . because I sincerely loved His poor, He taught me to know Him. . . . Better, let it be said that I found Him through His poor, and in a moment of joy I turned to Him."

*David Scott*
*Feast of St. Joseph the Worker*
*May 1, 2002*

# *About the Selections*

$\mathcal{T}$he selections in this book are all drawn from Dorothy Day's writings in *The Catholic Worker*. The selections are arranged simply according to some basic themes — finding the presence of Jesus in the Eucharist and in the poor; the ways and means of love; the transforming encounter with God in prayer, the Scriptures, and the sacraments; the witness of the saints and the universal call to holiness.

My purpose in selecting these texts and arranging them in this way is purely devotional. This is not intended as a systematic study of Dorothy Day's thought or spirituality. It should help anybody looking for the broad outlines of her thought and spirituality. But this is a devotional book. It is a book for those of us who want to draw from the spiritual wisdom of Dorothy Day in order to deepen our own faith and maybe even make some progress in our own spiritual lives. For the most part, I have chosen texts that can be prayed over and meditated on without any need for introduction or clarifying notes. In cases where people or things she refers to might not be readily known, I have included brief notes at the end of the book.

Also, Dorothy never included Scripture citations or identified the translations she was using or offered any sources for her many quotations from saints and other writers. And I have not felt it appropriate to clutter these selections with such citations or any type of critical or scholarly notations. I have rendered her Scripture quotes in *italic* and have made some stylistic changes for the sake of consistency.

One more thing: Dorothy Day did not cotton to the inclusive language that became fashionable in the last decade or two before her death. Occasionally in her later years she would throw in a line to appease some imagined critic: "When I say *men* I mean people, men and women." Once she wrote in exasperation: "All men are brothers (I refuse to be bullied into paraphrasing, and re-wording that beautiful saying into — 'all men and women are brothers and sisters')." I did not see any reason to contradict her wishes or to do any posthumous bullying of her beautiful and transcendent prose.

# I.

## *Practicing the Presence of God*

# *Introduction*

✠

*D*orothy Day's writings are shot through with a sharp sense of the personal presence of God hidden in the everyday. This, of course, is the good news of the Christian faith: that out of love God has entered human history, come in search of us, that He has taken on our flesh and remains living and active among us.

Jesus is the Holy One the prophets called Emmanuel, literally "God with us." And His promise was that He would never leave us orphans, that He would remain with us until the end of the age. Jesus said He would truly be with us when we gather to pray in His name, when we read the Sacred Scriptures, and when we partake of the sacraments, especially the sacrament of sacraments, the Eucharist. He said, too, that He would be present to us in His Church, His Mystical Body, and in the poor, the imprisoned, the least of our brothers and sisters.

Dorothy believed in the literal truth of these promises. But living among the poorest of the poor, she knew better than most of us that finding the presence of God in the people we meet, in the ordinary circumstances of our lives, is hardly something that comes naturally. To keep faith in His promise, to grow in this faith, Dorothy would say, takes the "supernatural" gift of God's grace, given in the sacrament of His presence, the Eucharist. It also takes "practice" on our part — daily acts of faith and devotion, self-sacrifice, and love.

*The selections that follow illustrate her conviction that the Eucharist is the great school of the divine presence and love. The daily encounter with Jesus in the Mass and in the tabernacle purifies and transforms us and should change the way we see things, the way we live. As we approach the altar and find that His flesh and blood are truly our food and drink, we will come to find His real presence in the flesh and blood of our family and neighbors, especially in the poor and the despised. And slowly, imperceptibly perhaps, we will begin to see fulfilled in our lives the promise of the Incarnation — God will begin to be for us, as He was for the Apostle Paul, "all in all."*

# Selections

✠

## Good Will Has Brought Us Here

If the heart is clear, a warm sunshiny day brings joy and health to the body. We do not think of the sun, we feel the warmth of the sun all about us, we feel it in the air, we see it reflected in people's faces, we can feel buds bursting on the trees in the parks.

It is like that to sit in the presence of the Blessed Sacrament in church. We do nothing, we don't think, or we have distractions, perhaps. The memory and understanding are feeble, but our good will has brought us there — our will to love and be loved. Christ there in the tabernacle, in His humanity and divinity, is like the sun acting upon us, healing us of our infirmities. We bathe ourselves in this sunlight which warms and heals us. *Lord, take away my heart of stone and give me a heart of flesh,* a warm heart that beats with Thy love.

*April 1935*[1]

✠

## Daily Communion: A Terrible Thing

What a terrible thing going to daily Communion is. . . . If we believe that Christ is present in the Blessed Sacrament of the altar, and He has invited us to come to Him and to partake of Him — then we are under this terrible obligation of obeying that Leader who we have accepted . . . and of being ready to accept the consequences of this daily act.

If we become daily communicants — if we are faithful in the observance of our religious duties, morning and evening prayer and frequent aspirations to place us in the presence of God during the day — then things are going to happen to us.

It is as though a dirty scroll were being washed so that we could read the writing thereon. Our very senses are going to be refined. We are going to be able to hear with our ears and see with our eyes and understand many things. St. Thomas said that he learned more by prayer than he did by study. We are going to be able to understand many things and the Lord is going to tell us what to do.

Just as the disciples prepared themselves by nine days of prayer for the descent of the Holy Spirit and His inspiration, so we must expect with hope that the Holy Spirit is going to enlighten us and lead us. We must expect the gifts of the Holy Spirit.

And the gift to be most afraid of is knowledge of what to do. Because if we know what to do, if our hearing has been sharpened and the Lord has spoken to us, and we do not pay attention, we are denying the inspirations of the Holy Spirit and we are failing in the virtues of faith, hope and charity. And if we keep on receiving inspirations and pay no attention to them for various reasons, then little by little that Voice will cease to speak, our hearts will be hardened, our senses deadened, graces will be withdrawn from us. And then as we continue to receive Our Lord daily in the Blessed Sacrament, religion will indeed become for us the opium of the people.

*July 1937*[2]

## Sensitive to the Spirit

You cannot receive the Blessed Sacrament without becoming sensitive to the inspirations of the Holy Spirit and these inspirations are to be put into practice. Do you know your neighbor in the first place? Or do you live in a neighborhood where nobody speaks to anybody else?

*February 1935*[3]

## Little Miracles

We live from day to day, and by the little miracles God performs in His bounty. *If we ask our Father for bread, will he give us a stone?* But ours is happiness, ours is joy, for Christ comes to us each day, not only at Christmas, but each time we look into the face of our brother who is poor.

*December 1952*[4]

✠
_____

## Because We Forget

It is because we forget the humanity of Christ — present with us today in the Blessed Sacrament just as truly as when He walked with His apostles through the corn-fields that Sunday long ago, breakfasting on the ears of corn — that we have ignored the material claims of our fellow man during this capitalistic, industrialist era. We have allowed our brothers and sisters, our fellow members in the Mystical Body to be degraded, to endure slavery to a machine, to live in rat-infested holes.

This ignoring of the material body of our humanity which Christ ennobled when He took flesh, gives rise to the aversion for religion evidenced by many. . . . As a result of this worshipping of the divinity alone of Christ and ignoring His sacred humanity, religious people looked to heaven for justice and Karl Marx could say, "Religion is the opium of the people." And Wobblies could say — "Work and pray, live on hay / You'll get pie in the sky when you die."

It is because we love Christ in His humanity that we can love our brothers. It is because we see Christ in the least of God's creatures, that we can talk to them of the love of God and know that what we write will reach their hearts.

*June 1935*[5]

## None for the Bums

A friend sent us a dollar yesterday, and with it the remark: "Enclosed is for bread, but not to make bums out of those who should be earning their own."

I thought of that this morning when I passed a little group of four who always seem to be hanging around the place, out in front, in the coffee room, in the doorways. Always drunk, sometimes prostrate on the sidewalk, sometimes sitting on the curb, they give a picture of despair or hilarity, according to the mood they are in. And, to the minds of many of our friends, they epitomize the six hundred or so who come here to eat every day.

This morning as I came from Mass, I passed the little vegetable woman around the corner, washing her mustard greens in a huge barrel of cold water. Her hands were raw and cold. It was one of those gray mornings, wet and misty, and the pavement was slimy under foot.

I commiserated with her over her hands, and she said: "What are you going to do? If you don't work, you don't eat." What a tradition of industry these Italians have — working steadily from morning to night, earning their income by pennies, and educating their children by those same pennies, even putting them through college.

When I passed this same little knot of men in front of the house whom I had passed on the way to church, I told them about the little Italian woman, and they hung their heads sheepishly and went away. I don't know what can be done — except to pray. Here are the most humiliated of men, the most despised, the evidence of their sins is flagrant and ever present. And as to what brought them to this pass — war and poverty, disease and sorrow — who can tell? Why question?

We must see Christ everywhere, even in His most degraded guise. We take care of men by the tens of thousands during the course of the year, and there is no time to stop and figure who are the worthy or who are the unworthy. We are each of us unprofitable servants. We are guilty of each other's sins.

*April 1943*[6]

✠

## Denying Christ in the Poor

One could weep with the tragedy of denying Christ in the poor. The Church is the Cross on which Christ is crucified and one does not separate Christ from His Cross, Guardini wrote.

Christ has left himself to us in the bread and wine on the altar; He has left himself to those who gather together, two and three in His name; He has left himself to us in the poor: *"There I am in the midst of you." "If you do it unto the least of these My brethren you do it unto Me." "I am Christ whom thou persecutest."* Saul was imprisoning and putting to death those who walked in the Way, and Christ cried out on the road to Damascus, *Saul, Saul, why persecutest thou Me?*

*July-August 1961*[7]

✠

## The Poor Are Your Masters

To help the poor! This is a great and fearful work. It is through the poor that we achieve our salvation; Jesus

Christ himself has said it in His picture of the last judgment. It is through the poor that we can exercise our faith and learn to love Him.

It is a great relief to read the lives of such saints as St. Vincent de Paul when doing this kind of work. An article some years ago said that he had contact with refugees, convicts, thieves, assassins and bandits, as well as with professional beggars, swindlers and prostitutes: "He saw quite clearly, and sometimes said, that many of these poor people were filthy, physically repulsive and suffering from loathsome diseases, that sometimes they were dishonest, drunken, hypocritical and ungrateful; but to use his own phrase, that is only one side of the medal. Turn it, and with the eyes of faith you see that each is stamped with the image of God and is a brother of Jesus Christ. . . ."

"The poor are your masters," he said, "and thank God you are allowed to serve them." We see in ourselves our measure of sin and decay of mind and body, but the more we can look at the good side of the coin, the better off we are ourselves, finding Christ. Our faith will grow through such an exercise of love.

*October 1964*[8]

## His Body and Blood, Our Food

If the Christ life is strong in us, if we are nourished daily by the food which is the body and blood of Christ, so that we are *putting off the old man and putting on Christ,* then we are able to find Christ in others, simply because He told us to, because He said of those we are

living with, *You are doing this to Me.* He said it, and our
faith, tried as though by fire, grows with exercise.

*August 1959*[9]

## Practicing Scales

I am convinced that daily Mass and Communion and
recitation of whatever part of the Office the busy layman
can achieve will result in a desire to live as closely united
to God as possible in "the practice of the presence of
God," to use Brother Lawrence's phrase, and the practice
of "praying without ceasing." The very word practice
brings with it the idea of learning. We practice scales on
the piano. And any practice is awkward and difficult.
But it is necessary to attain any kind of proficiency in the
spiritual life.

*February 1953*[10]

## He Will Do the Rest

We must practice the presence of God. He said that when
two or three are gathered together, there He is in the
midst of them. He is with us in our kitchens, at our tables,
on our breadlines, with our visitors, on our farms.

When we pray for our material needs, it brings us
closer to His humanity. He, too, needed food and shelter. He, too, warmed His hands at a fire and lay down in
a boat to sleep. When we have spiritual reading at meals,
when we have the Rosary at night, when we have study
groups, forums, when we go out to distribute literature

at meetings, or sell it on the street corners, Christ is there with us.

What we do is very little. But it is like the little boy with a few loaves and fishes. Christ took that little and increased it. He will do the rest. What we do is so little we may seem to be constantly failing. But so did He fail. He met with apparent failure on the Cross. But unless the seed fall into the earth and die, there is no harvest. And why must we see results? Our work is to sow. Another generation will be reaping the harvest.

*February 1940*[11]

✠

## His Homely Ways

It is the end of Easter week . . . and every day the epistles and Gospels have told the story of our risen Leader. On Monday there was the story of the two disciples traveling to Emmaus who did not recognize the stranger who was Our Lord until *they knew Him in the breaking of bread.* And then exclaimed joyfully, *Didn't our hearts burn within us when He talked to us?*

In another Gospel when the apostles were amazed at Our Lord's appearing to them, He said to them, *Have you anything to eat?* and sat down with them at dinner. Again, when He waited for them at the shore when seven of them were out fishing, He had a fire ready and cooked fish and they sat down together and ate.

What drew His followers so close to Him was the fact that He sat down and ate with them. He wandered in the fields with them plucking corn and eating. He was present at the wedding feast of Cana where He turned the water into wine. He cured Peter's mother-in-law of her fever and she got up and served them dinner. Martha busied herself cooking for the men coming together to discuss eternal things. When Jesus brought to life the little girl who had died, He told her mother, *Give her to eat.*

And when He talked of the final judgment, He said, *When I was thirsty, you gave Me to drink. When I was hungry you gave Me to eat. . . . Inasmuch as you have done it unto the least of My brethren, you have done it unto Me.* He expressed His love for us when He was here on this earth in homely ways. And He wants us to express our love for each other in those same ways. He said, *A new commandment I give unto you, that you love one another.*

*April 1937*[12]

### Give Back to Him

It is meant that we should be happy, that we should love the world *(for God so loved the world)*. Man has made a vast suffering wilderness of much of this world, through war and greed. But love is as strong as death. God said to St. Catherine of Siena: "You cannot give back to Me, myself, the love I demand, but I have put you beside your neighbor so that you may do for him what you cannot do for Me. What you do for your neighbor, then, I consider as being done for Me." He also said to her: "All the way to heaven is heaven, for I am the way."

*October 1946*[13]

## 'The Bourgeois Fat Lady'

One evening last week there was a man lying on the street pavement close up against our house, his knees up to his chest, his head on his arm. He was asleep. An Italian woman who could not speak English very well seized my arm as I came up. I could scarcely understand her, but she kept pointing to the man saying in turn, "Jesus Christ . . . my son, my heart is broken."

He wasn't really her son, but she knew what she was talking about. He *was* Jesus Christ, shocking as it may seem, drunk as he was. That was part of the agony in the garden, when He took our sins, and all the sins that would be committed upon himself.

People are always seeing this truth for the first time. Gandhi saw it when he read "Unto This Last" on a train ride, Ruskin's rendering of the Scripture words *unto the least of these*.

Salinger, the short story writer in *The New Yorker*, recognized it when the young brother in his latest story chided his sister for using the Jesus Prayer (famous in the Orthodox Church) for her own spiritual excitement, while she scoffed and scorned her neighbor. "Jesus," he tells her, "is the bourgeois fat lady on the porch in the rocking chair."

*November 1957*[14]

# Room for Christ

It is no use to say that we are born two thousand years too late to give room to Christ. Nor will those who live at the end of the world have been born too late. Christ is always with us, always asking for room in our hearts.

But now it is with the voice of our contemporaries that He speaks, with the eyes of store clerks, factory workers and children that He gazes; with the hands of office workers, slum dwellers and suburban housewives that He gives. It is with the feet of soldiers and tramps that He walks, and with the heart of anyone in need that He longs for shelter. And giving shelter or food to anyone who asks for it, or needs it, is giving it to Christ.

We can do now what those who knew Him in the days of His flesh did. I'm sure that the shepherds did not adore and then go away to leave Mary and her Child in the stable, but somehow found them room, even though what they had to offer might have been primitive enough.

All that the friends of Christ did in His lifetime for Him we can do. Peter's mother-in-law hastened to cook a meal for Him, and if anything in the Gospels can be inferred, it is surely that she gave the very best she had, with no thought of extravagance.

Matthew made a feast for Him and invited the whole town, so that the house was in an uproar of enjoyment, and the straight-laced Pharisees — the good people — were scandalized. So did Zacchaeus, only this time Christ invited himself and sent Zacchaeus home to get things ready. The people of Samaria, despised and isolated, were overjoyed to give Him hospitality, and for days He walked and ate and slept among them.

And the loveliest of all relationships in Christ's life, after His relationship with His Mother, is His friendship with Martha, Mary and Lazarus and the continual hospitality He found with them — for there was always a bed for Him there, always a welcome, always a meal.

It is a staggering thought that there were once two sisters and a brother whom Jesus looked on almost as His family and where He found a second home, where Martha got on with her work, bustling round in her house-proud way, and Mary simply sat in silence with Him.

If we hadn't got Christ's own words for it, it would seem raving lunacy to believe that if I offer a bed and food and hospitality for Christmas — or any other time, for that matter — to some man, woman or child, I am replaying the part of Lazarus or Martha or Mary and that my guest is Christ. There is nothing to show it, perhaps. There are no haloes already glowing round their heads — at least none that human eyes can see. . . .

It would be foolish to pretend that it is easy always to remember this. If everyone were holy and handsome, with "*alter Christus*" shining in neon lighting from them, it would be easy to see Christ in everyone. If Mary had appeared in Bethlehem clothed, as St. John says, with the sun, a crown of twelve stars on her head and the moon under her feet, then people would have fought to make room for her.

But that was not God's way for her nor is it Christ's way for himself now when He is disguised under every type of humanity that treads the earth. . . . For He said that a glass of water given to a beggar was given to Him.

He made heaven hinge on the way we act towards Him in His disguise of commonplace, frail and ordinary human beings.

*December 1945*[15]

---

## The Flesh of Mary

Our soul's life depends on our daily supersubstantial bread, Jesus Christ become incarnate, taking on our flesh through the flesh of Mary. Her assent: *Behold the handmaid of the Lord, be it done unto me according to Thy word*, is enough reason for our devotion to the Blessed Mother. . . .

After all, as St. Augustine said, "The flesh of Jesus is the flesh of Mary." If we love Jesus in His humanity (and the conversion of the two St. Teresas came about because of a sudden realization of it) we must love His Blessed Mother. When I say conversion I mean one of the many conversions we must all pass through. The saints themselves spoke of these experiences as conversions.

*June 1965*[16]

---

## Formed in Her Mold

Mary is present with us today, as yesterday and in every age. Two thousand years ago she gave us, through her flesh, our redeemer and God. She is the mold in which Christ was formed, and we in turn, her children, are in Mary being formed in the likeness of Christ. She is as close to us as the air we breathe.

*May 1954*[17]

# II.

## The Way of Love

# *Introduction*

*M*ade in the image and likeness of God who is love, we are born to love, Dorothy believed. For her, love is the meaning of life and it takes a lifetime to start to learn the real meaning of this love.

And yet like everything else in the Christian life, this love does not come easily. Dorothy was a realist. For her there was nothing soft and sentimental about love. She never tired of quoting the novelist Dostoyevsky: "Love in practice is a harsh and dreadful thing compared to love in dreams."

True love, to love as Jesus showed us how to love, is hard work, painful work. It means laying down your life, if not in literally dying for the ones you love, then in living wholly for their sake and the sake of God. To love is to offer your life as a gift, a sacrifice. It is to give yourself away without reserve to another, to God. Paradoxically, Dorothy wrote, what we suffer for love brings us untold joy.

As she shows us in the selections below, Dorothy believed that true love, in the end, is an act of faith. Because unless we believe in the promises of Jesus, it would be sheer madness to preach love in the face of so many people who seem so "unlovable," so many situations that are so "unlovely," in the face of a world that seems so ruthless, so devoid of love.

But love, by the grace of God, gives us new eyes, she said. We come to see people as God sees them, as God sees us — as infinitely precious, bought with the price of the blood of His Son. And by love we ourselves are transformed into the image of the One who made us, the God who is love.

# Selections

## Ten Meditations for Our Times

1. Love is the measure by which we shall be judged.
   — *St. John of the Cross*

2. Hell is not to love any more. — *Bernanos*

3. We can only show our love for God by our love for our fellows. — *St. Teresa*

4. How can we love God whom we do not see if we do not love our fellow human beings whom we see?
   — *St. John*

5. Love is a choice, a preference expressed by the will, *diligo,* so we can be commanded to love, to make choice of, to prefer God to all things. — *Bede Frost*

6. The soul that walks in love wearies not, neither is wearied. Love consists not in feeling great things, but in great detachment from things and suffering for the Beloved. — *St. John of the Cross*

7. Love is that of a bride for her husband.
   — *The Canticle of Canticles*

8. I love God as much as I love the one I love the least.
   — *Father Hugo*

9. Love in practice is a harsh and dreadful thing compared to love in dreams. — *Dostoyevsky*

10. To offer the other cheek, to love your neighbor as your-
    self, not because it pays to do so, but because it is a joy
    — to love him with fiery emotion, with passion!

*— Dostoyevsky*
*January 1944*[18]

✠

## The Eternal Theme

The love of God, this desire to grow in the love of God,
and the thought of the love of God for us, has been much
in my thoughts this past month of great feasts — the
feast of Corpus Christi and the feast of the Sacred Heart.

We cannot think of these feasts without thinking of
love and the desire of love. It is the common ground on
which we all meet. It is the eternal theme of Hollywood, it
is the subject of most of the pictures shown on Broadway
and Forty-second Street, taking it in its least common de-
nominator. It is so urgent a need of the human heart that
it seems a truism to say that it is the one thing that will
overcome all differences, even to the overcoming of wars.

*June 1951*[19]

✠

## What Else Do We All Want?

Whenever I groan within myself and think how hard it
is to keep writing about love in these times of tension
and strife which may at any moment become for us all a
time of terror, I think to myself: What else is the world
interested in? What else do we all want, each one of us,
except to love and be loved, in our families, in our work,
in all our relationships?

*God is love.* Love casts out fear. Even the most ardent revolutionist, seeking to change the world, to overturn the tables of the money changers, is trying to make a world where it is easier for people to love, to stand in that relationship with each other of love. We want with all our hearts to love, to be loved. And not just in the family but to look upon all as our mothers, sisters, brothers, children.

It is when we love the most intensely and most humanly, that we can recognize how tepid is our love for others. The keenness and intensity of love brings with it suffering, of course, but joy too because it is a foretaste of heaven. . . .

Even that relationship which is set off from other loves by that slight change in phraseology (instead of "loving," one is "in love") — the very change in terminology, denoting a living in love, a dwelling in love at all times, being bathed in love so that every waking thought, word, deed and suffering is permeated by that love — yes, that relationship above all should give us not only a taste of the love of God for us, but the kind of love we should have for all.

When you love people, you see all the good in them, all the Christ in them. God sees Christ, His Son, in us and loves us. And so we should see Christ in others, and nothing else, and love them. There can never be enough of it. There can never be enough thinking about it. St. John of the Cross said that where there was no love, put love and you would take out love. . . .

And this is not easy. Everyone will try to kill that love in you, even your nearest and dearest; at least, they will try to prune it: "Don't you know this, that and the other thing, about this person? He or she did this. If you don't want to hear it, you must hear it. It is for your good to hear it. It is my duty to tell you, and it is your duty to take recognition of it. You must stop loving, modify your loving, show your disapproval. You cannot possibly love — if you pretend you do, you are a hypocrite and the truth is not in you. . . ."

The antagonism often rises to a crescendo of vituperation, an intensification of opposition on all sides. You are quite borne down by it. And the only Christian answer is love, to the very end, to the laying down of your life. To see only the good, the Christ, in others.

*April 1948*[20]

✠

## To Prove There Is a God

One of the youngest members of our community, who is six, plays in the settlement house playground across the street and she came home a few weeks ago saying, "There is no God." This astounding fact had been passed on to her by one of the other children, who pointed out that, after all, they were deceived about Santa Claus, so why not about God?

The skeptic's little brother, who is four, told her earnestly that it was indeed true that there was a God, that after all, they had prayed for a baby and gotten it, and didn't that prove it? And where did all the babies come from anyway if there was no God? An irrefutable argument.

And as to how we are going to prove to the children that there is a God in this world of cold war, filled with the misery of the needy and the groaning of the poor, I can think of no better way than that of Julian of Norwich: "If a man love a creature singularly, above all creatures, he will make all creatures to love and to like that creature that he loveth so greatly."

We want to love God and how can we show it except by a love for His creatures. And the more they come and throng us, the more we should exert ourselves to show hospitality to these brothers of ours, these ambassadors of God. . . . And such service and such activity cannot be anxious, strained and unloving. It is the love which makes it easy and delightful and gives the strength and serenity to do all one has to do, in peace and quiet, as well as one can.

Christmas is a time for children especially and it is they who must be consoled and made happy and joyful. With all the problems of the world pressing on us, we are forced to be happy and loving with the children. No sense in darkening their lives with foreboding of the future or gloom over the present. Our very God himself comes to us at this time as a child, a baby, helpless and dependent, utterly defenseless and needing the comfort and support of others. . . .

And since we must go to Him at this season as to a baby in the stable, let us go to Him with gratitude and joy. St. Peter Chrysologus said: "The letter of a friend is comforting, but his presence is much more welcome; a bond is useful, but the payment is more so; blossoms are pleasing, but only till the fruit appears. The ancient fathers received God's letters, we enjoy His presence; they had the promise, we the accomplishment; they the bond, but we the payment." We are rich indeed.

*December 1949*[21]

✠

### Repay Love with Love

Our God is indeed a *personal* God to whom it is fit and proper that we bring our praise and petitions. He has first called us and He has first loved us, and we have a duty and a joy to repay love with love.

*July-August 1950*[22]

✠

## An Exchange of Gifts

Peter Maurin likes to emphasize the Christianity inherent in some of our slogans, such as "What can I do for you?" sometimes with joking truthfulness turned into, "What can I do you for?"

It certainly is a solution to the world's problem, this idea of looking around to see what you can do for those around you, a true expression of the second commandment, and the only way we have of showing our love for God whom we have not seen by our love for those whom we do see. "Love is an exchange of gifts." And "love is the measure by which we shall be judged."

*December 1942*[23]

✠

## Come, Let Us Begin

One of the saints says that we can only measure our love of God by our love of our neighbor. If we love him we wish to serve him, protect him, we wish him to feel our love. Think of the love of a mother for her child. Is there anything she would not forgive that child? Is there anything that God will not forgive us? We are His children.

St. Francis used to say every day, "Come, let us begin to love God." "Now I have begun," is the motto of another religious order. Every morning or at anytime during the day we can lift our hearts and say, "Now I have begun."

Is not this faithfulness, Lord, to turn and turn again to Thee and say, "Fill the hearts of Thy faithful with Divine Love"? In regard to this faithfulness, "We have been faithful to Thee in our fashion," we say wryly. . . . But after all, *Thou knowest that we are but dust.*

"Prayer is the desire of the heart, and the heart knows well how to desire." So we will not count our prayers on beads, nor try to gauge our love in measuring cups, but only open our hearts to God's love which we feel and know and believe in with every breath we draw.

*April 1935*[24]

## Think of His Love

St. Teresa talks of the necessity of not thinking of our love of God, but of His for us. His love is so vast, so permeating, it is like sunlight. We must open our hearts to it. Contemplating the love of God, our hearts are filled with, not our own, but His love. It is His love which irradiates our hearts. We cannot by ourselves love Him or our neighbor. We can only abandon ourselves to His love. *Thou knowest we are but dust. God so loved us that He gave His only begotten Son.*

*April 1935*[25]

## A Foolish Love

And I thought too of the kind of love we should have for each other, a love which discounted the irascible remark, a confident love, a love which at times might look like folly indeed.

What more foolish a love is there than that portrayed in the Gospel — the father for the prodigal son, the love of the shepherd for his sheep, the love which asked the servants to sit down so that the Master could minister to them, wash their feet in a gesture of total and utter abandonment of love! And how far we are from it all!

*April 1949*[26]

## To Learn Such Folly

It is an easy thing to talk about love, but it is something to be proven, to be suffered, to be learned. I remembered the Book of Hosea, the prophet and holy man who was commanded by God to love and marry a harlot, who had children by him, and who left him again and again, having children also by her lovers.

And how Hosea again and again took her back. How he must have been scorned by his generation, he a holy man, so weak and uxorious, so soft-minded that again and again, "he allured her" to him, on one occasion even buying her back from her lover, even providing her, while she was with her lover, with corn and wine and oil.

And God even commanded it so that down through the ages there would be this example of God's love for a faithless people, of the folly of love, a foretaste of the folly of the Cross. If we could only learn to be such fools! God give us the strength to persist in trying to learn such folly.

*April 1948*[27]

## A Perfect Fool for Christ

We knew a priest once, a most lovable soul, and a perfect fool for Christ. Many of his fellow priests laughed at him and said, "Why, he lines up even the insane and baptizes them. He has no judgment!" He used to visit the Negro hospital in St. Louis, and night and day found him wandering through the wards. One old Negro said to me, "Whenever I open my eyes, there is Father!"

He was forever hovering over his children to dispense the sacraments. It was all he had to give. He couldn't change the rickety old hospital, he couldn't provide them with decent housing, he could not see that they got better jobs. He couldn't even seem to do much about making them give up liquor and women and gambling — but he could love them, and love them all, he did. And he gave them everything he had. He gave them Christ. Some of his friends used to add, "whether they wanted Him or not!" But assuredly they wanted his love and they saw Christ in him when they saw his love for them.

Many times I have been reminded of this old priest of St. Louis, this old Jesuit, when I have visited prisons and hospitals for the insane. It's hard to visit the chaplains and ask their help very often. They have thousands to take care of, and too often they take the view that "it's no use." "What's the use of going to that ward — or to that jail? They won't listen to you."

If one loves enough one is importunate, one repeats his love as he repeats his Hail Marys on his Rosary. . . . What does the modern world know of love, with its divorces, with its light touching of the surface of love? It has never reached down into the depths, to the misery and pain and glory of love which endures to death and beyond it. We have not yet begun to learn about love. Now is the time to begin, to start afresh, to use this divine weapon.

*June 1946*[28]

✠
———

## As God Sees

St. Augustine said that we should always love everyone as though he or she were the only one. If we saw people as God sees them, we should indeed see the beauties of each unique soul. And if we had the love of God in us we would indeed be seeing them as God sees them.

*June 1965*[29]

✠
————————

## Through a Glass Darkly

And I thought, how mighty was man's love, how tremendous a force, how transforming a power. And how wonderful it would be if our love for God, not just the desire to love God, were so strong that it would overflow into our work for many of our brothers (and all men are brothers). . . .

To be in love is to begin to have some knowledge of the love of God. It is the way we should love everyone, each person we encounter. It is seeing all as God sees them — as unique, lovable. In other words, it is a foretaste of heaven. It is the more abundant life which Christ talks of. And yet there is so much suffering involved in it. We are unhappy with the suffering and the grief of loved ones; our own hearts ache, almost physically, and we are often heavy with sorrow. . . .

Yes, we love our own selves, and we love our own, our families, our children, but it is often a love of self extended; it is not the love of God which we have glimpsed, which we have seen reflected in love of brother or love of country, or love of the Church, which strengthens men to the greatest sacrifices and endurance. It is seeing through a glass darkly, as St. Paul says, but we do get glimpses of this so mysterious love.

*January 1969*[30]

✠

---

## A Harsh and Dreadful Thing

But of course it is hard to love our fellow man. Father Zossima in *The Brothers Karamazov* said, "Love in practice is a harsh and dreadful thing compared to love in dreams." He was talking of a great humanitarian who said the further away from people he was, the more he could love them.

There are some people whom it is easy to love. God in His goodness has given the heart of man the capacity for human love, and it is good to compare the love between a betrothed man and woman and the love we are to bear each other. Love makes all things easy. When one loves, there is at that time a correlation between the spiritual and the material. Even the flesh itself is energized, the human spirit is made strong. All sacrifice, all suffering is easy for the sake of love.

A mother will endure all-night vigils by the bedside of a sick child. With every child that is born to her, born in anguish that is quickly forgotten, an all too small a price to pay, her heart is enlarged to take another in. Strength and endurance and courage are granted to her with the love she bears those near and dear to her. When we hear of parents failing in this faithfulness, we are repelled as by something "unnatural."

If love can be so great, and we must remember that grace builds upon nature, then how great should be the supernatural love we should bear our fellows? It is this love which will solve all problems, family, national, international. . . . Love intensifies the natural joys of life, the comradeship we have for one another, the little joys of meals together, work together, the sunlight which warms us and the rain and mist which nourish the ground which bears our daily bread. . . .

We walk by faith and not by sight, as St. Paul said, and we see things through a glass darkly. But we do know that love fulfills the law and that love is the measure by which we shall be judged. So though we feed thousands every day, if we haven't love we have accomplished nothing. We live with wayfarers and the lame, the halt and the blind, but if we just shelter them, feed them and clothe them and do not love them, it is nothing. We go out on picket lines and distribute literature, to try to bring the message of Christ and His love to the workers who are lost to the Church, but if we work without love, it is in vain. Let us pray then that the love of God will increase in our hearts and that this desire to love be strengthened in us.

*May 1939*[31]

## Love Is an Act of Faith

St. Teresa said that you can only show your love for God by your love for your neighbor, for your brother and sister. . . . But how to love? That is the question. All men are brothers, yes, but how to love your brother or sister when they are sunk in ugliness, foulness and degradation, so that all the senses are affronted? How to love when the adversary shows a face to you of implacable hatred, or just cold loathing?

The very fact that we put ourselves in these situations, I think, attests to our desire to love God and our neighbor. . . . It has always required an overwhelming act of faith. I believe because I wish to believe. *Help Thou my unbelief.* I love because I want to love, the deepest desire of my heart is for love, for union, for communion, for community. How to keep such desires, such dreams? Certainly, like Elias, who, after making valiant attempts to do what he considered the will of God, fled in fear, all courage drained from him, and lay down under a juniper tree and cried to God to make an end of his misery and despair.

The grace of hope, this consciousness that there is in every person that which is of God, comes and goes, in a rhythm like that of the sea. *The Spirit blows where it listeth,* and we travel through deserts and much darkness and doubt. We can only make that act of faith, "Lord, I believe because I want to believe."

We must remember that faith, like love, is an act of the will, an act of preference. God speaks, He answers the cries in the darkness as He always did. He is incarnate in the poor, in the bread we break together. We know Him and each other in the breaking of bread.

*May 1978*[32]

## Offering Ourselves

We love and worship and adore and thank the God we acknowledge as our Creator. We owe Him that as creatures. Only our life itself is sufficient homage. But we cannot take our own lives as a sacrifice to God, as an offering of ourselves. We acknowledge that we belong to God, that He owns us, not we ourselves. He possesses us. . . .

Only the God who made us has the right to take our life. So in worship we offer that which is the equivalent of our life, bread and wine, that which feeds us and becomes bone of our bone, flesh of our flesh.

*June 1951*[33]

## The More You Love

The more you love in this life, the more you suffer, and yet who would be without love? God is love, the beatific vision is love; in Him we possess all things.

*March 1952*[34]

## We Must Become Like Him

In the old and new testaments there are various ways in which the relationship of God and men are mentioned. There is the shepherd and his sheep. *The Lord is my shepherd. I am the Good Shepherd.* The animal and the man. There is the servant and the master, there is the son and the father, and there is the bride and the bridegroom. *Behold, the bridegroom cometh.* The Song of Songs, the

Canticle of Canticles, is all about love. *Let Him kiss me with the kisses of His mouth.* It is hard to believe in this love. . . .

The love of God and man becomes the love of equals as the love of the bride and the bridegroom is the love of equals, and not the love of the sheep for the shepherd, or the servant for the master, or the son for the father.

We may stand at times in the relationship of servant, and at other times in that of son, as far as our feelings go and in our present state. But the relationship to which we hope to attain, is that of the love of the Canticle of Canticles. If we cannot deny the self in us, kill the self love, as He has commanded, and put on the Christ life, then God will do it for us. We must become like Him. Love must go through purgations.

*September 1948*[35]

✠

---

## A Leper Learns of Love

Father Roy, our dear Josephite friend who worked with us at Easton and who has been these past two years in a hospital in Montreal learning what it is to be loved, used to tell a story of a leper he met at a hospital up on the Gaspé Peninsula; the leper complained to him, "How could he believe in the love of God?"

Father Roy proceeded to tell his favorite story. First of all there is dirt, the humus from which all things spring, and the flower says to the dirt, "How would you like to grow and wave in the breeze and praise God?" and the dirt says "Yes," and that necessitates its losing its own self as dirt and becoming something else.

Then the chicken comes along and says to the flower, "How would you like to be a chicken and walk around like I do, and praise God?" and the flower assures the chicken that it would like it indeed. But then it has to cease to be a flower.

And the man comes to the chicken and says to it, "How would you like to be a man and praise God?" and of course the chicken would like it too, but it has to undergo a painful death to be assimilated to the man, in order to praise God.

When Father Roy told this story he said with awe, "And the leper looked at me, and a light dawned in his eyes, and he clasped my hands and gasped, 'Father!' And then we both cried together."

Father Roy is a childlike man, and the Russian leper up in the Canadian peninsula was a simple sufferer, and he saw the point that Father Roy was trying to make and he began to believe in this love, and to see some reason for his sufferings. He began to comprehend the heights and the depths, and the strange mystery of this devouring love. But it still takes the eyes of faith to see it.

*September 1948*[36]

✠

## Love Came Down to the Mire

It grows ever harder to talk of love in the face of a scorning world. We have not begun to learn the meaning of love, the strength of it, the joy of it. And I am afraid we are not going to learn it from reading the daily papers or considering the struggles that are taking place on the other side of the world and in the United Nations halls here at home.

We are the little ones, and we can only pray to the saints of our days, the little saints, to disclose to us this hidden world of the Gospel, this Hidden God, this pearl of great price, this kingdom of heaven within us. It is only then can we learn about love and rejoicing, and it is the meaning of life and its reward.

We talk of one world, and our common humanity, and the brotherhood of man, of principles of justice and freedom which befit the dignity of man, but from whence does he derive this dignity but that he is the son of God?

The one lesson which is reiterated over and over again is that we are one, we pray to be one, we want to love and suffer for each other, so let us pray and do penance in each little way that is offered us through the days, and God will then give us a heart of flesh to take away our heart of stone and with our prayers we can save all those dying each day, knowing that God will wipe away all tears from their eyes.

Lest these words which I write on my knees be scorned, know they are St. John's words, the apostle of love, who lived to see "charity grow cold" and who never ceased to cry out, "My children, love one another." It is the only word for Christmas, when love came down to the mire, to teach us that love.

*December 1950*[37]

## The New Way of Love

Christ commanded His followers to perform what Christians have come to call the Works of Mercy: feeding the hungry, giving drink to the thirsty, clothing the naked, sheltering the harborless, visiting the sick and prisoner, and burying the dead.

Surely a simple program for direct action, and one enjoined on all of us. Not just for impersonal "poverty programs," government-funded agencies, but help given from the heart at a personal sacrifice. And how opposite a program this is to the works of war which starve people by embargoes, lay waste the land, destroy homes, wipe out populations, mutilate and condemn millions more to confinement in hospitals and prisons.

At the Last Supper . . . Christ washed the feet of His Apostles. He came to serve, to show the new Way, the way of the powerless. In the face of Empire, the Way of Love.

*May 1972*[38]

☩

## Mother of Fair Love

This is Our Lady's month and we turn to her especially now in this time of life and growth and blossoming and we turn to her especially to teach us how to love. It is what we are here for, it is why God has given us our life. The two commandments of life are to love God and to love our neighbor. We are here to love.

The great problem of the day is to build up this love, to feed it, to strengthen it, to make it grow into the force that can overcome hatred and war. . . . The one thing to pray for is to learn to love. Love is wisdom and wisdom is the most active of all active things.

"Not death itself is so strong as love, not the grave itself cruel as love unrequited; the torch that lights it is a blaze of fire. Yes, love is a fire which no waters avail to quench, no floods to drown; for love, a man will give up all that he has in the world and think nothing of the loss."

And who epitomizes this love so well as the Blessed Mother, from whom we received Love itself, a Love which died for us. . . . When old Bill Duffy lay dead on the floor beside his bed, it was Christ himself who lay there dead, Christ in one of His least. He has said this to us and we have to believe it and it is a terrible thought, a terrible exercise of our faith. We begin to realize how we need to pray to love each one near to us with whom we sit down to eat.

"We love God as much as we love the least," Father Hugo said once, and it is a way of examining our conscience as to how much we love. When our life is over we will be examined as to how much we have loved and it is on this that we will be judged.

Grave crimes are being committed throughout the world; there is torture and slavery and cruel death, there is deceit and lying and hate, and we are not being ostriches, hiding our heads in the sand when we repeat that we must see Christ in His most degraded guise, we must see Him in all men and we must pray to learn to love. If we do this, then we can be sure, as St. John of the Cross said, "Where there is no love, put love and you will take out love."

Mary, mother of fair love and of fear and of knowledge and of holy hope, pray for us. Pray that God will take away my heart of stone and give me a heart of flesh to suffer and to love. In this is all grace of the way, all delight.

*May 1950*[39]

# III.

## Weapons of the Spirit: Prayer, the Bible, and the Sacraments

# Introduction

✠

*I*t is usually remarked that Dorothy Day had a very "traditional" Catholic piety. And it is true that she lived by the rhythms of the Church's seasonal calendar and its liturgy for the hours of the day. She went to Mass every morning and spent time in adoration before the Blessed Sacrament every day. Despite a busy schedule of work and travel, she found time to pray the Rosary, study the Scriptures, and practice contemplative prayer each day. She went to confession every week.

For Dorothy these were not obligatory habits or rote rituals. For her, prayer, the Bible, and the sacraments were all ways of drawing near to the living God, all ways that the living God draws near to us. As she shows in the selections below, for her these are "weapons of the Spirit," given to us by Jesus in His Church to help us in our daily struggles, our seeking after meaning and transcendence. They are the means by which God in His grace builds up the divine life inside us, bringing us deeper into the life of the Trinity and bringing the life of the Trinity deeper into our own lives.

Through these means Jesus purifies us, makes us holier, day by day transforms us into the kind of person that God intends us to be: children made in the image of our Father in heaven, creatures of His love, filled with His Spirit, called to follow in the footsteps of His Son, the true image of God and the true image of the human person. Or, as Dorothy Day says with St. Paul, "other Christs."

# Selections

## Prayer for a Change

Dear God, let us not accept that judgment —
   that this is what we are.
Enlighten our minds, inflame our hearts with the desire
      to change —
   with the hope and faith that we all can change.
Take away our hearts of stone and give us hearts of flesh.

*July-August 1972*[40]

## The Lonely Revolution

The revolution we are engaged in is a lonely revolution, fought out in our own hearts, a struggle between nature and grace. It is the most important work of all in which we are engaged.

If we concentrate our energies primarily on that, then we can trust those impulses of the Holy Spirit and follow them simply, without question. We can trust and believe that all things will work together for good to them that love God, and that He will guide and direct us in our work.

We will accomplish just what He wishes us to accomplish and no more, regardless of our striving. Since we have good will, one need no longer worry as though the work depended just on ourselves.

*December 1934*[41]

✠

## He Asks Us to Do Just a Little

We have been reading the story of the Pilgrim who learned to pray without ceasing, and since reading it, we notice how that theme recurs over and over in the Mass.

It is necessary to pray "at all times and in all places," it reads at the beginning of the Preface of the Mass. . . . Over and over again, *without ceasing,* we should call upon God. *Ask and it shall be given you, seek and you shall find, knock and it shall be opened to you. . . .*

We none of us can do very much for each other, and really, it seems that God does not expect very much of us. He asks us each to do just a little, and He will do the rest. He asks us to give our mite, like the widow's; our few loaves and fishes, like the little boy's; our handful of meal, like the widow's; our mess of pottage like Habakkuk's; He asks us to wash in the Jordan, a simple cure in the face of so gigantic a physical evil as leprosy.

He asks us to do just a little, and then He takes hold and does the rest. He will do the rehabilitating, in His own good time. He will change the heart, taking away the heart of stone. He will comfort the afflicted and give strength to those all but overcome by moral conflicts.

*April 1953*[42]

✠

## Prayer for Beginners

And here I am living on the beach, writing, answering some letters, and trying to grow in the life of the Spirit. I feel that I am but a beginner. I am convinced that the life of prayer, to pray without ceasing, is one of prime importance.

Years ago, Father Wendell, a wonderful Dominican priest in St. Vincent Ferrer's parish in New York, came to us one summer every Wednesday night and talked to us about prayer.

One simple sentence he pointed out has remained in my memory these last twenty-five years. Something for beginners, he said, and God knows we are always, each morning, beginning again! "Remember the word *ACTS*," he said, "and that those initials stand for Adoration, Contrition, Thanksgiving and Supplication, and you will have a very simple method of praying."

*March-April 1975*[43]

## No Prayer Too Small

There is nothing too small to pray about. "O God, come to my assistance; O Lord, make haste to help me." Sometimes one is so tired, so dull, so hopeless, that it is a great effort of the will to remember to pray even so short a prayer. *O Lord, hear my prayer. Let my cry come unto Thee. . . .*

I must write about prayer because it is as necessary to life as breathing. It is food and drink. . . . Prayer is an *exercise*, sometimes dull, sometimes boring, but it brings health to the soul, which needs exercise just as the body does.

*July-August 1973*[44]

## To Say the 'Our Father'

Often I am tempted to depression, thinking that I have scarcely begun to live a spiritual life, even to live the way we all profess to, that of voluntary poverty and manual labor. . . .

But, just to say over and over again that one prayer, the *Our Father*, is to revive, to return to a sense of joy.

"The worst malady of all is sadness," caused by lack of trust in the Lord and the desire to impose our own will on Him. Pope John wrote this in one of his letters to his family. In another place, there is this — "I repeat: to know how to say the *Our Father*, and to know how to put it into practice, this is the perfection of the Christian life." He gives me courage and, believing in "the communion of saints," I pray to him often.

*September 1975*[45]

✠

## Helpless But for Prayer

A few years ago an old woman died in our midst, here at our House of Hospitality in New York. She was surrounded by many men and women she had known a long time; she had the best of care.

We had a nurse living with us who could meet any emergency. But Catherine, the last few weeks of her life, often clutched at my hand as I passed her, and would plead with me, "There is a God, tell me there is a God! Tell me!"

I could only say, "Yes, Catherine, there is a God. He is our Father and He loves us, you and me." When you say these things it is an act of faith. You feel your help-lessness so you pray harder. You seem to know nothing; you can only hold her hand and make your affirmation.

So much of our prayer is made up of these affirmations. "I praise Thee, O God, I bless Thee. What have I on earth but Thee and what do I desire in heaven besides Thee?"

I am saying this *for* Catherine, *instead* of Catherine, because she is in "the valley of the shadow." But did I comfort her? A few days later a young girl said to me, "The word *Father* means nothing to me. It brings me no comfort. I had a drunken father who abused my mother and beat his children."

We can do nothing by our words. So we are driven to prayer by our helplessness. God takes over.

*March-April 1976*[46]

✠

## Waiting for the Light to Change

As I waited for the traffic light to change on my way to the Seamen's Defense Committee headquarters, I was idly saying my Rosary, which was handy in my pocket. The recitation was more or less automatic, when suddenly like a bright light, like a joyful thought, the words *Our Father* pierced my heart.

To all those who were about me, to all the passersby, to the longshoremen idling about the corner, black and white, to the striking seamen I was going to see, I was akin, for we are all children of a common Father, all creatures of one Creator, and Catholic or Protestant, Jew or Christian, communist or non-communist, were bound together by this tie.

We cannot escape the recognition of the fact that we are all brothers. Whether or not a man believes in Jesus Christ, His Incarnation, His life here with us, His Crucifixion and Resurrection; whether or not a man believes in God, the fact remains that we are all the children of one Father.

*November 1936*[47]

✠

---

## Praying with Christ

The basis of the liturgical movement is prayer, the liturgical prayer of the Church. It is a revolt against private, individual prayer. St. Paul said, *We know not what we should pray for as we ought, but the Spirit himself asketh for us with unspeakable groanings.*

When we pray thus we pray *with* Christ, not *to* Christ. When we recite Prime and Compline we are using the inspired prayer of the Church. When we pray with Christ (not to Him) we realize Christ as our Brother.

We think of all men as our brothers then, as members of the Mystical Body of Christ. *We are all members, one of another,* and, remembering this, we can never be indifferent to the social miseries and evils of the day. The dogma of the Mystical Body has tremendous social implications. . . .

Many people confuse liturgy with rubric — with externals. Again . . . when we pray in this way we recognize the universality of the Church; we are praying with white and black and men of all nationalities all over the world. . . .

Living the liturgical day as much as we are able, beginning with Prime, using the Missal, ending the day

74

with Compline and so going through the liturgical year we find that it is now not us, but Christ in us, who is working to combat injustice and oppression. We are on our way to becoming "other Christs."

*January 1936*[48]

✠

## There Is No Time with God

*In the sight of the unwise they seemed to die, but they are in peace.* This is a verse which always brings comfort. We all have a long list of the dead to pray for, relatives and friends.

So many of mine are non-Catholics, and I have always remembered the advice of an Augustinian priest years ago. "There is no time with God," he said, "and all the prayers you will say for those souls were as though you said them before their death, and God always answers prayers. Who knows what graces He offered them at the moment of death, or at that instant after when the soul is released from the body."

*November 1946*[49]

✠

## A Mother's Prayer

That evening I was driving Becky, Susie, Eric and Nickie to the store and they started quarrelling while I was doing the shopping so that when I came out, tears were streaming down cheeks and there were wails about who kicked whom.

In desperation I said, exercising the priesthood of the laity, "We will all now make a good act of contrition

— O my God, I am heartily sorry for having offended Thee and I detest all my sins, my fightings, and quarrelling, and harsh words and kickings. . . ."

There was complete silence and suddenly a great calm descended. Peace was restored. And I thought with intense gratitude: Oh, what would we do without prayer, without faith, without our guardian angels to help us!

*May 1954*[50]

✠
———————

## Of Guardian Angels

I am so firmly convinced of their existence to this day that I pray to them daily.

*June 1967*[51]

✠
———————

## The Jesus Prayer

Sometimes the house is like the reception ward at Bellevue Psychiatric. One can only bow one's head to the storm and pray. The Jesus Prayer helps me.

*June 1973*[52]

✠
———————

## Repeating Prayer

Thank God for short repetitious prayer. Gandhi said that he used to repeat the name of God over and over again to give himself courage. The Russian Orthodox believe that even invoking the Holy Name of Jesus results in His presence with you. And there are all the prayers to the Blessed Mother, short and swift like arrows.

Of course, all those who say, "Lord, Lord," are not going to receive a blessing, unless they go out and try to do the will of the Father. But the very doing of that will may mean a stammering in our prayers. And when we cannot pray, if we cannot lift up our hearts, others will be doing it for us. We are all members one of another. We are all guilty of the sins of the world, and we all lift each other up.

*October 1955*[53]

## Hail Mary

These beautiful words which we repeat so often throughout the day are the words of an angel and the words of Elizabeth. . . . A phrase of such prayer sufficed the saints often to raise them to heights of contemplation.

At the same time it is hard to understand why people object to repetitive prayer, when our natural life too is made up of such repetitive acts as breathing. "Doth it not irk Me that upon the beach the tides monotonous run? Shall I not teach the sea some new speech?" (Sister Madeleva).

*July-August 1954*[54]

## Make Haste to Help Us

Patience, patience. I often reflect that the word itself means suffering. *Take up your cross and follow Me.* But, *My yoke is easy, My burden light,* Jesus said. You learn what He meant only if you keep praying about it. *O God, make haste to help us!*

*September 1974*[55]

## Pay God a Compliment

You pay God a compliment, St. Teresa of Ávila says, by asking great things of Him. And God is good. Even without our asking. . . . As Teresa, an activist, said, "Teresa and three ducats can do nothing, but God and Teresa and three ducats can do everything." And God returns to the giver a hundredfold.

*October-November 1973*[56]

## The 'Gimme' Novena

We are not at all abashed at saying that we are indulging in what is generally termed a "gimme" novena. We are told to ask by Jesus himself. *Ask and you shall receive, seek and you shall find, knock and it shall be opened to you.*

This novena is generally termed the Rosary novena. For three novenas (nine days each) you ask for what you need in temporal and spiritual favors. And then whether or not you have received your request, you start three more novenas in thanksgiving.

It takes, you see, fifty-four days and I do know that before the time is up you are overwhelmed with favors of one kind or another. I would be so bold as to say you really get your request! And here is the kind of a story that infuriates those who term us superstitious.

My acquaintance with the Rosary novena began back in 1937 when one of the girls who came to help us with the children we were taking care of for the summer began to make it to get herself a husband.

She had met someone she loved and so she started to pray. Every night, before she went to sleep, when the dormitory of sleeping children was a bit of heaven and the smell of sweet clover filled the barn where we lived, she would sit with her dark head bent under the oil lamp and pray her beads with the little blue book in her hand. In the fall she was married.

So I started saying it in order that we might purchase the farm which adjoined the hill-top farm we had bought the year before. The price was four thousand dollars and we needed a thousand to make a down payment, the butcher-owner holding a mortgage on the rest. He was a Syrian separated from his wife, who lived in Lebanon.

Before I was through the first two novenas a donation of a thousand dollars came in to make our down payment. I was so overjoyed and so dizzy with success that I probably started the end before I finished the beginning.

Anyway, to buy the place, the signature of both husband and wife were needed, that being the law of Pennsylvania. So Mr. Boulous, the butcher, signed the deed, and sent it to his wife, who signed it in beautiful Aramaic, which was the script of Our Lord's day, and had it notarized and sent back to Easton, Pennsylvania.

It took a time, and when it came, it was defective and had to be sent back to Lebanon, far over the seas to the Near East. Weeks passed, months passed, and somehow the money that came in for the farm was all eaten up; it had been frittered away in grocery bills, because the work of feeding people, after all, is never done, but goes on and on three times daily, day after day, and will go on as long as we shall live.

When I realized that the money had been spent, was no longer in the bank, I girded my loins and started another Rosary novena. Before the first three novenas were over and done, once again a thousand dollars had come in. . . . (We do assure you that such offerings are few and far between. I cannot remember when the last one came.)

*May 1950*[57]

&#10013;

## A Prayer to the Little Flower

One afternoon this summer, three little children and I were walking through the fields, and they showed me a cross in the field over which were growing clusters of grapes. We stopped to say a prayer, and I suddenly thought to pray for the $500 we needed to make a payment on the mortgage the following week. That very evening a friend came to us and told us he had the money for our use.

God answers prayers. This we know. But He answers them through you . . . and through the saints who watch over our work.

The chapel on the farm at Staten Island is named for the Little Flower, so we say to her: "Remember your happy life at home, your good father and mother and how you used to go fishing and walking and picnicking, how you celebrated the feast days of the Church. Help us, too, to make others happy, because when people are happy, then it is easier for them to be good. Help us to make a garden, an oasis, a little bit of heaven here where love dwells. Where love is, there God is."

*October 1951*[58]

## Three Prayers for Strength

May I suggest these three acts of faith, hope and charity, quotations from Scripture which should strengthen us? *Lord, I believe, help Thou my unbelief. In Thee have I hoped, let me never be confounded. Dear Lord, take away my heart of stone and give a heart of flesh,* so I may learn to love, to grow in love.

*July-August 1973*[59]

## Done Enough?

There is a terrible saying a priest once quoted to us, "He who says he has done enough, has already perished."

If we went daily to our local church, and there, in the presence of Christ, brought our problems, our pain, our suffering at our failures, and our mistakes which contribute so much to the sufferings of others, then I think we would be more nearly doing "enough." The growth of prayer groups all over the country does not mean a slackening of the struggle for peace and justice, but a strengthening of it.

*October-November 1972*[60]

## Prayer for Love

Pray with me that men be joined together in love,
    so strong a love in their march Godwards,
    that they will draw all with them,
    that all suspicion, anger, contention, bitterness and
      violence

be burnt away in the fire of this love.
And may it open their eyes,
   the brightness of this love,
   to the works we can all perform together
   in building up a new society,
   in our work for food, clothing, shelter, education
      and health
   for all men,
   for these are the works of mercy, of love and not of
      hate,
   the works of good, not evil, of God, not the Devil.
And where there is no love, put love and we will find
      love;
   because love is the measure by which we shall be
      judged.

*January 1963*[61]

## His Name Is Honey

So let us all, with St. Paul, *rejoice in the Lord always,* re-membering Christ's beatitudes and call on the name of the Lord — recalling too St. Bernard's words: "Jesus is honey in the mouth, music to the ear, a shout of gladness in the heart" — because Christ, our Incarnate God, is present in His name and in His word, even as He was in the cloud which went before the Israelites.

*June 1974*[62]

✠

## Kissing the Book

I have recently read Chaim Potok's books — all of them — with the greatest interest. . . . One line in Potok: "I wonder if Gentiles clasp Holy Scripture in their arms and dance with it, as we Jews do?" Well, I've often seen people kiss the Book before and after reading it, and I do myself.

*September 1977*[63]

✠

## Word Power

One day we were sitting out under the trees and I was reading to the children the epistle and Gospel of the day, and talking to them about the potency of the Word of God, how holy Scriptures were, what a blessing they brought to those who read them, and how when the Word of God was preached by St. Francis and St. Anthony all the birds of the air and all the fish of the sea came closer to hear.

And as I spoke and as I read we looked at the little chipmunks and there they were, suddenly quiet, no longer racing madly up and down the cage, standing on their heads and performing for us, but they were poised, motionless on the branches inside the cage, their bright little eyes alert and watchful.

*December 1955*[64]

## Special Message for Our Need

Even if we read only the Gospel for Sunday, several times, God sends us a special message for our need.

*July-August 1953*[65]

## Songs of Solace

I turn most truly for solace, for strength to endure, to the Psalms. I may read them mechanically at first, but I do believe they are the Word, and that Scripture on the one hand and the Eucharist, the Word made flesh, on the other, have in them that strength which no power on earth can withstand.

*June 1972*[66]

## Reading Fire

"Attend to reading," St. Paul said to Timothy. St. Jerome writes to Eustochium, "Let sleep creep over you holding a book and let the sacred page receive your drooping face."

St. Augustine said, "Do you know how we should read Holy Scripture? As when a person reads letters that have come from his native country, to see what news we have of heaven."

Rodriguez says that reading is sister and companion to meditation.

St. Jerome wrote, "Where is this fire? (of the love of God). Doubtless in the Holy Scriptures, by the reading whereof the soul is set on fire with God and purified from all vices." St. John 6:63: *The words that I have given you are spirit and life.*

## Reading As Prayer

This type of reading is a form of prayer. The little St. Thérèse used to read the Scriptures constantly (in those days she was permitted to read only part of the Old Testament, so we Catholics can rejoice in the freedom we have now, even though we recognize that freedom is dangerous, imposing terrible responsibilities on us to try to live as we believe and profess).

Often this reading the Scriptures is like plodding through a desert, we get so little from it. And then chapters, verses, shine out with a great light and our way is made clear for us.

Yes, reading is prayer — it is searching for light on the terrible problems of the day, at home and abroad, personal problems and national problems, that bring us suffering of soul and mind and body. And relief *always* comes. A way is always opened, *Seek and you shall find.*

*July-August 1973*[68]

## Searching for Light

I cannot write and express myself without using the words and phrases of St. Paul, of Scripture. We are told to *search the Scriptures* to find comfort and guidance.

St. Thérèse of Lisieux, who reminds me of Brother Lawrence in her practice of the "little way," said once that she could read fifty chapters of Isaiah and get nothing out of them and then suddenly the fifty-first flooded her soul with light. Which makes me think of the subconscious mind working away, and leaping on what it needs for sustenance, comfort, or understanding.

*March-April 1976*[69]

## No Pulpit for Politics

St. Teresa said she so loved to hear the Word of God preached that she could listen with enjoyment to the poorest preacher. I know what she meant. Just as long as it is the Word of God, and not politics, finances and labor discussions from the altar. On the first Sunday in Lent our Italian priest spoke to us on "too much eatings, too much drinkings," and how we should make our souls strong. He was very simple and very good.

*March 1939*[70]

## It All Seems So Clear

It all seems so clear, when you go to Communion each day and read the Bible, receiving the Word of God made Flesh and the Word of God.

*February 1958*[71]

## Believe in the Sacraments

I believe in the Sacraments. I believe grace is conferred through the Sacraments. I believe the priest is empowered to forgive sins. Grace is defined as *participation in the di-*

*vine life*, so little by little we are putting off the old man and putting on the new. Actually, *putting on Christ.*

*December 1972*[72]

✠

## All the Great Moments of Life

A great wave of gratitude to Holy Mother Church swept over me as I thought of the ministrations of these priests. At nine there had been the colorful and solemn and most happy occasion of all the little children of the parish making their first Holy Communion. And at ten this Mass for the dead!

All the great moments of life are here clothed with grandeur, recognition of man's dignity, his worth in the sight of God who loved him so much as to die for him. First Communion coming to young ones at a time when the desires of the flesh begin to grow, opening up their hearts to a love strong as death, showing them what love really means.

St. Thérèse called her first Holy Communion "a kiss of love, a fusion." And now a requiem Mass which brought comfort to the afflicted, a sense of triumph. Death is swallowed up in victory. . . .

I thought too of those who attacked the Church which so recognized our dignity and brought us such gifts . . . who attack the Church not knowing her, and prayed for them.

We know that through her priests we receive our rebirth in Christ, our communions, our healings of soul and body. She witnesses our marriages and helps us to die, and our priests are ordained for these great and noble duties of bringing to us the sacraments, the means of grace which enable us to begin to truly live.

All this morning I was witnessing the regard Holy Church had for man, her recognition of his humanity. This ceremony can be done without, though it is a fitting clothing, and has been done without in mission countries and in times of persecution.

But these ceremonies are an outward and visible sign, as the sacraments are, of the love which fills our lives, just as the marriage act is a sign of love, a kiss, an embrace, a tenderness, even a smile, all these are earthly things, which mean much more than the act itself. We are creatures of body and soul and those who reject Christ are rejecting the body and this life here and now. . . .

There is always the danger, I thought, of the real significance of things being lost in the Martha-business of daily life. But . . . for us all, the curtain is lifted now and again, and we see, as through a glass darkly, the great things that God has prepared for those who love Him.

*June 1954*[3]

---

### Forget Birthdays

We have been celebrating everyone's name day and baptismal day lately and have decided to forget birthdays forever. Newman said that were it not for the life of grace, the birth of a child into the world would be a most tragic event. We can easily understand that, considering the state of the world today. . . .

"The vow promised in Baptism is the greatest and most indispensable of all vows," says St. Augustine. "The principal source of all disorder among Christians comes from forgetfulness and indifference about the vows of their Baptism; hence the best remedy for these disorders is the sincere renewal of these vows." (Council of Sens)

*June 1946*[74]

✠

## The Seed of Divine Life

In a book by Hugh of St. Victor which I read once on the way from St. Paul to Chicago, there is a conversation between the soul and God about this love. The soul is petulant and wants to know what kind of a love is that which loves all indiscriminately, the thief and the Samaritan, the wife and the mother and the harlot?

The soul complains that it wishes a particular love, a love for herself alone. And God replies fondly that after all, since no two people are alike in this world, He has indeed a particular fondness for each one of us, an exclusive love to satisfy each one alone.

It is hard to believe in this love because it is a devouring love. It is a terrible thing to fall into the hands of a living God. If we do once catch a glimpse of it we are afraid of it. Once we recognize that we are sons of God, that the seed of divine life has been planted in us at baptism, we are overcome by that obligation placed upon us of growing in the love of God. And what we do not do voluntarily, He will do for us.

*September 1948*[75]

✠

## Christ Is Living Water

A flood of water (and Christ is living water) washes out sins — all manner of filth, degradation, fear, horror. He is also the Word.

And studying the New Testament and its commentators, I have come, in this my 76th year, to think of a few holy words of Jesus as the greatest comfort of my life: *Judge not. Forgive us our trespasses as we forgive those who trespass against us. Forgive seventy times seven times.* All words of Our Lord and Savior.

*I have knowledge of salvation through forgiveness of my sins,* Zechariah sang in his canticle. And so, when it comes to divorce, birth control, abortion, I must write in this way. The teaching of Christ, the Word, must be upheld. Held up though one would think that it is completely beyond us — out of our reach, impossible to follow.

I believe Christ is our Truth and is with us always. We may stretch towards it, falling short, failing seventy times seven times, but forgiveness is always there. He is a kind and loving judge. And so are 99 percent of the priests in the confessional.

The verdict there is always "not guilty" even though our "firm resolve with the help of His grace to confess our sins, do penance and amend our lives" may seem a hopeless proposition.

It always contains, that act of contrition, the phrase "to confess our sins," even though we have just finished confessing them, which indicates that the priest knows, and we know, and we want to be honest about it, that we will be back in that confessional, again and again.

*December 1972*[76]

✠
―――――――――――

### Where Is the Confessional?

The seventy-times-seven teaching of Jesus about forgiveness . . . marks the power of the confessional. But where is the confessional these days? We want a place where we can hide our heads as we confess our mean and paltry sins.

*October-November 1975*[77]

✠
_____

## Confess We Are Seeking Christ

Nowadays when there are no longer lines at the confessionals in our churches except at the business district's noonday Masses, there surely is an overflowing of public confessions.

In our newspapers, reviews, advertisements and novels "nothing is hidden, it seems, that has not been revealed." It is as though the fear of death, and judgment day has made people rush to tell all, to confess to each other, before the dread Judge shall tell all to the universe.

Poor, fearful creatures that we are, is it that in this strange perverse way of confessing we are seeking Christ, even those who deny Him? Jesus Christ is our truth. By telling the truth, or one aspect of the truth, perhaps we are clinging to the hem of His garment, seeking to touch it like the woman with the *issue of blood*, so that we may be healed.

*December 1972*[78]

✠
_____

## The Heart of Our Life

This is probably my last chance . . . personally to write about some things that are in my heart about the Mass . . . that Holy Sacrifice, which is the heart of our life, bringing us into the closest of all contacts with Our Lord Jesus Christ, enabling us literally to *put on Christ,* as St.

Paul said, and to begin to say with him, *Now, not I live, but Jesus Christ in me.* With a strong consciousness of this, we remember too those lines, *without Me, you can do nothing,* and *with Me you can do all things.*

We know through long experience how hard it is to think in these terms, and only through constant exercise in the works of love and peace can we grow in faith, hope and charity. Only by nourishing ourselves as we have been bidden to do by Christ, by eating His body and drinking His blood, can we become Christ and put on the new man.

These are great mysteries. Most of the time we do not comprehend at all. Sometimes the Holy Spirit blows upon us and chases some of the fog away and we see a bit more clearly. But most of the time we see through a glass darkly.

Our need to worship, to praise, to give thanksgiving, makes us return to the Mass daily, as the only fitting worship which we can offer to God.

Having received our God in the consecrated bread and wine, which still to sense is bread and wine, it is now not we ourselves who do these things except by virtue of the fact that we will to do them, and put ourselves in the position to do them by coming to the Holy Sacrifice, receiving Communion, and then with Christ in our hearts and literally within us in the bread we have received, giving this praise, honor and glory and thanksgiving.

How inadequate words are to say these things, to write them. . . . The Mass begins our day, it is our food and drink, our delight, our refreshment, our courage, our light.

*September 1962*[79]

## The Power of Mere Words

With this recognition of the importance of the Word made flesh and dwelling among us, still with us in the bread and wine of the altar, how can any priest tear through the Mass as though it were a repetitious duty? . . .

The priest often says the first words and slides through the rest in meaningless mutter. And some of the best priests I have met do this, abusing the prayers of the Mass in this way.

I am begging them not to. I am begging them to speak as though the words were holy and inspired and with power in themselves to produce in us the understanding — the participation that should change our lives.

"You cannot fail to see the power of mere words," Joseph Conrad wrote in his preface to *A Personal Record.* "Such words as Glory, for instance, or Pity. Shouted with perseverance, with ardor, with conviction, these two by their sound alone, have set whole nations in motion and upheaved the dry hard ground on which rests our whole social fabric."

*September 1962*[80]

✠

## A Romantic Traditionalist

I am afraid I am a traditionalist, in that I do not like to see Mass offered with a large coffee cup as a chalice. I suppose I am romantic too, since I loved the Arthur legend as a child and reverenced the Holy Grail and the search for it.

I feel with Newman that my faith is founded on a creed, as Father Louis Bouyer wrote of Newman in that magnificent biography of his. "I believe in God, Father Almighty, Creator of heaven and earth. And of all things visible and invisible, and in His Only Son Jesus Christ, Our Lord."

I believe too that when the priest offers Mass at the altar, and says the solemn words, "This is my body, this is my blood," that the bread and the wine truly become the body and blood of Christ, Son of God, one of the three Divine Persons. I believe in a personal God. I believe in Jesus Christ, true God and true man.

And intimate, oh how most closely intimate we may desire to be, I believe we must render most reverent homage to Him who created us and stilled the sea and told the winds to be calm, and multiplied the loaves and fishes. He is transcendent and He is immanent. He is closer than the air we breathe and just as vital to us. I speak impetuously, from my heart, and if I err theologically in my expression, I beg forgiveness. . . .

We begin the Mass by the confession of sins, admitting our creatureliness, and all the beginnings of disorder that there are in us, and part of our thanksgiving is because of the forgiveness of sin and we do not dwell on falls and failures but go swiftly on to the prayers of praise and adoration and thanksgiving.

To me the Mass . . . is glorious and I feel that though we know we are but dust, at the same time we know, too, and most surely through the Mass, that we are little less than the angels, that indeed it is now not I but Christ in me worshipping, and in Him I can do all things, though without Him I am nothing.

I would not dare write or speak or try to follow the vocation God has given me to work for the poor and for peace if I did not have this constant reassurance of the Mass, the confidence the Mass gives. (The very word confidence means "with faith.")

It is one thing for a Father Ciszek to offer Mass, to consecrate the wine in a coffee cup in the prison camps of Siberia. It is quite another thing to have this happen in New York.

And yet — and yet — perhaps it happened to remind us that the power of God did not rest on all these appurtenances with which we surround it. That all over the world, in the jungles of South America and Vietnam and Africa — all the troubled, indeed anguished spots of the world — there Christ is with the poor, the suffering, even in the cup we share together, in the bread we eat. *They knew Him in the breaking of bread.*

*March 1966*[81]

✠

---

## So-Called Folk Masses

I have just come from a glorious celebration, the eleven o'clock Mass at St. Thomas the Apostle Church. . . . It was a special Lenten Mass composed by Mary Lou Williams and is being sung every Sunday during Lent by the entire congregation, led by the young people's singing group. . . .

One came away feeling as though one had truly celebrated Mass, offering worship, adoration, glory to God, not to speak of penitence. The prayers sung and recited are very much to the point.

At the *Kyrie Eleison* the choir sings, "For my lack of hope," and the congregation answers, "Lord, have mercy." And the petitions are repeated, "For my lack of faith, for our failure to care, for letting ourselves be paralyzed with fear, for our divisions, for our jealousies, for our hatred, for not being peacemakers, for our lies — Lord, have mercy on my soul."

There is a climax of beauty at the singing of the choir, after the *Sanctus* — "Dying, You destroyed our death; Rising, You restored our life. We will sing of You until You are seen by all the world."

As for the *Great Amen*, which is still more or less ignored by all our local churches, it is hard to describe the ecstatic, "Glory to God, to Jesus Christ," and the half dozen repeated Amens followed by a final strong one sung by the entire congregation.

This was a musical event, and I do not think there has been anything to compare with it in any of the so-called folk Masses being sung in colleges and churches around the country. The setting of devotional words to swinging, popular tunes may make an appeal to many but there can be no comparison with the music we heard today.

*March 1968*[82]

## New Masses

Here is a gem I found in C. S. Lewis' *Letters:*

> "The advantage of a fixed form of service is that we know what is coming. Extempore public prayer has this difficulty: we don't know whether we can join in it until we've heard it — it might be phony or heretical. We are therefore called upon to carry

on a critical and devotional activity at the same moment, two things hardly compatible.

"In a fixed form we ought to have gone through the motions before in our private prayer; the rigid form really sets our devotions free. I also find that the more rigid it is, the easier to keep our thoughts from straying. Also it prevents getting too completely eaten up by whatever happens to be the preoccupation of the moment, war, and election or whatnot.

"The permanent shape of Christianity shows through. I don't see how the extempore method can help but become provincial and I think it has a great tendency to direct attention to the minister rather than to God."

C. S. Lewis "speaks to my condition," as the Quakers say. Which leads me into reflections on the new Masses, the intimate Masses, the colloquial Masses, the folk-song Masses, and so on. . . .

There is also the attempt made by some young priests to reach the young, to make the Mass meaningful to the young (the bourgeois, educated, middle-class young) where novelty is supposed to attract the attention but which, as far as I can see, has led to drawing these same young ones completely away from the "people of God," "the Masses" and worship in the parish church.

There is the suggestion of contempt here, for the people, and for the faith of the inarticulate ones of the earth, "the ancient lowly" as they have been called. Their perseverance in worship, week after week, holy day after holy day, has always impressed me and filled my heart with a sense of love for all my fellow Catholics, even Birchites, bigots, racists, priests and lay people alike, whom I could term "my enemies," whom I am bidden to love.

Our worst enemies are of our own household, Scripture says. We are united, however, as people in marriage are united, by the deepest spiritual bond, participation in the sacraments, so that we have become "one flesh" in the Mystical Body.

I do love the guitar Masses, and the Masses where the recorder and the flute are played, and sometimes the glorious and triumphant trumpet. But I do not want them every day, any more than we ever wanted solemn Gregorian Requiem Masses every day. They are for the occasion. . . .

They are joyful and happy Masses indeed and supposed to attract the young. But the beginning of faith is something different. *The fear of the Lord is the beginning of wisdom.* Fear in the sense of *awe.*

*May 1967*[83]

✠

_____

### The Work of Our Salvation

It is joy that brought me to the faith, joy at the birth of my child, 35 years ago, and that joy is constantly renewed as I daily receive Our Lord at Mass. At first I thought that following the prayers of the Mass would become monotonous and something for the priests to continue day after day, and that was why people were silent and bookless.

Some Quakers going to Mass with me once said, "Now I know what the Mass is, it is a meditation." But it is an act, a sacrifice, attended by prayers, and these prayers, repeated daily, of adoration, contrition, thanksgiving, supplication, are ever there. One or another emotion may predominate, but the act performed evokes the feeling of "performing the work of our salvation."

*January 1962*[84]

## To Save Our Brothers

Daily Mass and Communion are so necessary now that it is as though we were neglecting to save our brothers, reach them a helping hand in their agony, when we omit going. . . . Praying in unison with others, corporate prayer, ascending before the throne of God, is one great means we have in our power to bring relief. . . .

We have got to look for sacrifices we can make, we have to examine our consciences for self-indulgences each day, we have got to feel more and more the absolute necessity for daily Mass and Communion offered up for our brothers in agony.

*June 1940*[85]

## Mass on a Hill of Junk

I encountered Mexicans across our border in a most miserable condition of destitution, living in rags on these dumps managed by a contractor, who paid the Mexicans to scavenge for old iron, metals, bottles and other trash. The average family, with all members working, could earn barely enough to feed themselves.

It was on the top of this hill of junk that a small, cement-block shed with no windows, only open spaces, was their little chapel. Benches were built from bits of lumber. A confessional had been set up, perhaps constructed from the wreck of an old car, and there men and women went to confession, while those left in the chapel sang their joyous hymns and awaited the Mass.

After the Eucharist there was a sharing of clothes brought by the group from El Paso, and a small grocery cooperative was set up where hundred-pound sacks of beans and rice made up the produce.

It was a long and beautiful morning. It was not just social work. It was a sharing, a visit, a day of festival. . . . The El Paso group was giving the best they had and they paid their Mexican brothers and sisters the compliment of recognizing that they too rejoiced in the primacy of the spiritual.

*October-November 1975*[86]

⁜

## He Must Be Our Food

God so loved the world that He gave His only begotten Son. And that Son loved God and us, His brothers, so that He lay on the altar of the Cross and sacrificed His life for us in worship and atonement.

He was our life gaining for us eternal life. Showing us the way of love and surrender, suffering and death. So He must also be our food, our bread and wine, our meat indeed. This is literally true.

The flesh of Jesus is the flesh of Mary, St. Augustine says. He is man as we are with all our strivings, labors, fatigues, temptations. When we take Him, His life, His flesh and blood, we become Him.

We drink our mother's milk from her body. Her blood nourishes us as we lie in her womb. Mary's blood nourishes Christ, and His blood nourishes us. He drank from her body and became man. We eat His body and drink His blood and become God. It is reasonable for us to believe this but we cannot understand it.

*June 1951*[87]

## Anointed Hands

Yesterday while I prayed in our parish church, there was a baptism going on, and I thought how close the priests were to our hearts — how they came to us in all the most holy and happy moments of our lives, birth and death and marriage, with the life-giving sacraments which their anointed hands alone could bring.

*April 1949*[88]

## The Priest's True Work

To him Mass was truly *the work* of the day and he spared no effort to make it as beautiful and worshipful as possible. Even during the coldest weather when the water froze in the cruet and his hands became numb, he said Mass slowly, reverently with a mind intent on the greatness, the awfulness of the Sacrifice.

To one priest who complained of his powerlessness to cope with the darkness of the times, he said courageously (it is hard to correct a priest about so personal a matter) that if he would stop gargling the words of the Mass in his throat in a horrible parody of oral prayer, he would be making a beginning. That same priest who was also a sensitive soul never again slurred over the words of the Mass. . . .

He emphasized the fact that the maniple used to be a cloth over the arm to wipe away the sweat and the tears of the first priests offering up the Holy Sacrifice and said that when we had participated in this great work of the day we had done the most we could possibly do.

But Father Roy's Mass once offered did not prevent him from being a most diligent worker. He had what Peter Maurin called a philosophy of labor. He took great joy in it and counted any day lost that did not see some heavy manual work performed. He felt he could not eat his bread without having shed some sweat. . . .

In addition to saying his Office, he spent an hour of adoration and in order to make us share this hour he urged us to go to the chapel right after breakfast to pray.

*November 1954*[89]

## The Communion of Marriage

The love of mother and child, the love of brother, the love of husband and wife! When we love we wish to be so taken by the one loved that we are consumed, we are identified with him, we become one, and this is the communion of marriage. It is what marriage strives for.

Yet no matter how perfect the marriage, no mortal man or woman can be satisfied with less than God. "Our hearts were made for Thee and find no rest until they rest in Thee." We see Christ in each other, and when we love most generously we see Christ more intensely. But it is still through a glass darkly, and not face to face.

*June 1951*[90]

---

### Death of a Homeless Man

His weakness increasing, when he returned to the emergency section, Arthur and a friendly nurse got him a stretcher to lie on so that he would not have to continue sitting up on a hard bench.

Surrounded by the usual rush all about, Arthur was able to talk to him about praying. "Do you know the *Confiteor?*" he asked him. "Do you know the act of contrition?" and he helped the man say them. "Do you want a priest?" and the man eagerly assented, and thank God the priest was near at hand and came at once. He was anointed, given absolution, and it was not more than an hour after that that he died.

When we consider the power of the Sacrament, the infinite value of the Precious Blood shed for this man in the Redemption, and remember too the story of the good thief and the promise of Christ, we can rejoice that this man is in heaven.

Sometimes we can only realize the grandeur of our human destiny, our divinization through baptism, when we hear the strains of some great music like Beethoven's *Ninth Symphony*, or his *Eroica*, or Strauss's *Death and Transfiguration*, the very title of which inspires.

It is hard to realize the worth of human life surrounded as we are by the Bowery and the Lower East Side, and that section of it which is more than ever crowded due to the tearing down of so many homes to eliminate slums. Thank God for His mercy, His love for each human soul.

*November 1956*[91]

✠

## For a Good Death

When I was saying the *Our Father* and the *Hail Mary* this morning, it suddenly occurred to me how good it was to end our prayer to Mary with "now and at the hour of our death."

I don't think I had ever realized how often we pray for the hour of our death, that it would be a good one. It is good, certainly, to have a long period of "ill health". . . nothing specific, mild but frightening pains in the heart, and sickness, ebb-tide, ebbing of life, and then some days of strength and creativity.

*June 1977*[92]

✠

## Joy of Love, Come to Us

Yet if we feel the misery of others more keenly than we do our own, if we have said to God in the words of Mary, *Be it done unto me according to Thy word*, if we suffer for others so that we are driven to prayer for them, then that joy of love comes to us — a joy which is alive and vital and filled with hope even in the midst of sorrow.

One cannot love without being warmed by that love. "Love is the measure by which we shall be judged," St. John of the Cross said, and to obtain that love, knowledge of God and knowledge of man is necessary. Love without such knowledge is but sentimentality and condescension.

We know God more and more by living with Him, and we know the poor in whom He is with us today, by living with them. And that knowledge and that love come also to us through our Mother who is the "mother of fair love, of fear and of knowledge and of holy hope."

Mary will give us humility so we will acknowledge the littleness of what we do. We can say, "Lord, my heart is not lifted up nor are mine eyes lofty. Neither have I walked in greater matters nor in things too wonderful for me."

If we have this humility, we will depend more on prayer, recognizing the primacy of the spiritual. If this is our aim, we can remember with courage, "The saints through faith subdued kingdoms, wrought justice."

The miracle of the marriage feast of Cana is one of the happiest stories in the New Testament. Through urging Our Lord to perform the miracle of supplying wine for the festivity some writers say that Our Lady started Our Lord out in His public life.

She gave Him to us in the first place by her consenting, *Be it done unto me according to Thy word.* The flesh of Jesus became the flesh of Mary, as St. Augustine reminds us. And the first miracle He performed was at her instigation.

The meditation written by the Hungarian Bishop Prohaszka interprets this incident thus: "The feast of our life is often very sad," he writes. "There is much heavy food which science and politics provide, but our wine is missing, which should refresh the soul and fill it with pure noble joy of life. Oh, our Mother, intercede on our behalf with thy divine Son. Show Him our needs, tell Him with trust: They have no wine. He will provide for us. . . . Sweet wine, fiery wine, the Lord Jesus gives to our bridal soul; He warms and heats our hearts. Oh, sweet is the wine of the first fiery love of the first elating zeal."

Let us ask our Mother for this elating zeal, in this time of the world's sorrow.

*May 1940*[93]

# IV.

## To Be a Saint

# Introduction

✠

*D*orothy Day wanted to be a saint. Not necessarily an officially canonized saint of the Church, but a holy woman, a woman transfigured by her faithful response to the call of Jesus, by her imitation of Christ.

Decades before the Second Vatican Council restated with such beauty and force the ancient Catholic belief that God calls each of us to holiness and perfection, Dorothy Day was living it and preaching it. She liked to repeat the lines from the French novelist and polemicist Leon Bloy: "There is only one sadness, and that is not to be one of the saints."

In the selections that follow, Dorothy looks to the canonized saints as sources of new vitality and renewal in the history of the Church, and as personal friends and intercessors — guides and models for her own life. In the saints she saw the fulfillment of the promise of the Incarnation — that because God became flesh in Jesus, our flesh, our lives, and everything we see and touch and say and do, can become of God, filled with His presence, offered in thanksgiving for His glory.

# Selections

✠

---

## Can't Change Human Nature?

You hear people say, "You can't change human nature." So it is good to keep in mind that prayer in the Mass: "O God, who in creating human nature, didst marvelously ennoble it, and hast still more marvelously renewed it; grant that, by the mystery of this water and wine, we may be partakers of His divinity, who vouchsafed to become partaker of our humanity."

*September 1933*[94]

✠

---

## We Are Raised to Divinity

She did not wait until Christ had been brought forth before she set out as an apostle. On hearing the Word, she arose and went with haste and visited Elizabeth her cousin, who was with child also, about to give birth to that great apostle known as St. John the Baptist.

Our Lady of the Visitation is the patroness, for us, of lay apostles. The Holy Ghost overshadowed her, she conceived by the Holy Ghost, she is the spouse of the Holy Ghost and she is the Mother of God — a profound mystery.

What we do understand is that "the flesh of Jesus is the flesh of Mary," as St. Augustine said, and He shared our human nature because she consented with her *fiat* that He should. God made subject to man — an inconceivable humility. We who are "native to nothingness" are raised to divinity by this sharing. The seed of divine life is planted in us by our baptism.

*July-August 1954*[95]

## When God Wants a Saint

"It is all God's doing," St. Thérèse, the Little Flower, points out in her autobiography. "When God wants a saint, He makes one." Of course the person in question has to give assent. I wondered how many there are who have been *called to be saints* and have refused because the price was too great?

*June 1965*[96]

## They Can Put a Man on the Moon . . .

These days I can never look up at the sky and see the moon without thinking with wonder and awe that men have walked there. To conceive of such a thing — to desire such an adventure, to be capable of overcoming all fear, all doubt, to have faith in man's ability to solve problems, and seek out the way to go about this great exploration — what dedication of mind and will! *What is man that Thou are mindful of him? Thou hast made him little less than the angels.*

It keeps coming into my mind — how much man would be capable of if his soul were strong in the love of God, if he wanted God as much as he wanted to penetrate the power and glory of God's creation.

To know Him, to love Him and to serve Him — a personal God, who took on human flesh and became man and suffered and died for us. To find the way, not to the moon but to God — this is man's real desire, because of his need for love, and God is love.

*March-April 1976*[97]

## Called to Be Holy

In the old translation of Scripture, St. Paul greeted people in his letters as *called to be saints*. And wrote also that we should put off *the old man* and *put on Christ. Be ye therefore holy.* In other words "whole men," developing all our faculties — spiritual, mental and physical.

When I think how men have walked on the moon — their courage, their faith — how highly developed their mental and physical capacities, I feel we are woefully underdeveloped spiritually.

*June 1974*[98]

## A Joyful Doctrine

Oh, the joyful doctrine of the communion of saints!

*May 1956*[99]

## Who Are the Saints?

The saints were those who did understand concerning the needy and the poor. All they could see was that Jesus Christ, true God and true man, came to this world where such horror exists, and died for each and every one. . . .

The saints are those who knew how to love, whose lives were transformed by love. The desire deep in the heart of every one of us, is to love, to love in such a way that all things become new, that there is a new song in our hearts. St. Augustine says we must learn to love everyone as though we loved him alone most particularly in all the world. St. Paul says we are *called to be saints. . . .*

The saints were in such harmony with all created things that the very animals loved them and loved to be with them. They shed around them an aura of love because they had put off the old man and put on Christ. . . . There is sung each Sunday, the definition of the blessed:

> *Blessed are ye poor for yours is the kingdom of God.*
> *Blessed are ye that hunger now; for you shall be filled.*
> *Blessed are ye that weep now; for you shall laugh.*
> *Blessed shall ye be when men shall hate you, and when they shall separate you, and shall reproach you and cast out your name as evil, for the Son of Man's sake. Be glad in that day and rejoice: For behold, your reward is great in heaven.*
> *November 1955*[100]

## On the Scene in All Bad Times

I always liked to read about saints. In all bad times of luxury and corruption in the Church, there was always a St. Francis, a St. Anthony, a St. Benedict, a Vincent de Paul, a Teresa and a Thérèse on the scene to enliven history.

*June 1974*[101]

## 'Cranks' and 'Trouble Makers'

We talk about the saints and are thrilled by the idea of sanctity, but the question is, how would we react to a St.

Francis, a St. Benedict Joseph Labré, a Curé of Ars? Human respect is one of the greatest stumbling blocks.

I repeat: We would not recognize the saint if we met him on the street corner today. He would be "the crank," the "unbalanced," the "trouble maker," etc.

*April 1950*[102]

### Scandal and Fuss

His own monks tried to poison St. Benedict and there was scandalous behavior within the monastery itself, as a protest then against the so-called rigor of the saint. There must have been an awful fuss made too when St. Francis insisted on offering up the Holy Sacrifice at Christmas in a stable.

*February 1967*[103]

### Seekers Among the Poor

All the saints have begun their mission by seeking Christ among the poor.

*November 1951*[104]

### Giving All to the Poor

The baby was born at twelve-thirty, a boy, eight pounds, James Matthew by name. The hospital called it Thursday, but by God's time, not daylight saving, the child was born on the feast of St. Lawrence, always one of my favorite saints. When there was danger of the estates of the Church being confiscated by the State, he sold them all and gave them to the poor! A good example for our time.

*September 1949*[105]

### How Much Has God Given You?

St. Augustine has some good advice about voluntary poverty which enables us all to do the works of mercy. "Find out how much God has given you, and from it take what you need; the remainder which you do not require is needed by others." The superfluities of the rich are the necessities of the poor. Those who retain what is superfluous possess the goods of others.

*October-November 1971*[106]

### The Blood of the Poor

One way to keep poor of course is not to accept money which is the result of defrauding the poor. Here is a story of St. Ignatius of Sardinia, a Capuchin just canonized last October. Ignatius used to go out from his monastery with a sack to beg from the people of the town but he would never go to a merchant who had built up his fortune by defrauding the poor.

Franchino, the rich man, fumed every time he passed his door, at being so neglected, though this perhaps seems even more unbelievable than the climax of the story. His concern, however, was not the loss of the opportunity to give an alms, but the fear of public opinion. He complained at the friary, whereupon the Father Guardian ordered St. Ignatius to beg from the merchant the next time he went out.

"Very well," said Ignatius obediently. "If you wish it, Father, I will go, but I would not have the Capuchins dine on the blood of the poor."

The merchant received Ignatius with great flattery and gave him generous alms, asking him to come again in the future. But hardly had Ignatius left the house with his sack on his shoulder than drops of blood began oozing from the sack. They trickled down on Franchino's doorstep and down through the street to the monastery. Everywhere Ignatius went a trickle of blood followed him.

When he arrived at the friary he laid the sack at the Father Guardian's feet. "What is this?" gasped the Guardian. "This," St. Ignatius said, "is the blood of the poor."

*May 1952*[107]

✠

---

### To Give to the Thief

There was a wayfarer . . . who stole the Thanksgiving turkey out of the refrigerator at Mott Street years ago and there was hullabaloo over that!

I think it was then that I thought of St. John Cantius, who ran after the thief who was making off with his wallet to tell him that there was still a gold piece tied up in his cloak, whereupon the thief fell on his knees in repentance and gave back what he had taken. . . .

I did not have much faith in this story however. . . . Just the same . . . ten years later, when we had moved to Chrystie Street, that same thief came in one day and gave whoever sat at the desk a ten dollar bill, saying it was in restitution for a turkey he had walked off with years before.

*February 1964*[108]

## Be What May Be

Thoughts on holy silence: St. Gregory kept silence during Lent. Holy Abbot Agatho for three years carried a pebble in his mouth to gain the virtue of silence. Abbot Deicoola always had a smile on his face and when asked why he was so happy, he said, "Be what may be and come what may come, no one can take God from me."

*March 1945*[109]

## Cheerfulness and Charity

St. Apollo formed a community of 500 monks near Hermapolis, who received daily Communion and listened to a daily homily. In these he often insisted on the evils of melancholy and sadness, saying that cheerfulness of heart is necessary amidst our tears of penance as being the fruit of charity, and requisite to maintain the spirit of fervor. He himself was known to strangers by the joy of his countenance.

*March 1945*[110]

## A Message to the World

On February 27 in the lives of the saints there seemed to be an abundance of hermits: Thalaleus who lived in a penitential cage and wept continuously, round about the year 450; St. Baldmerus, a more attractive figure, also a hermit, whose one message to the world was, "always give thanks to God." The wild birds used to come and eat from his hands, and he told them too, "Take your refreshment and always bless the Lord of heaven."

*March 1958*[111]

## Where Love Is

We ask you in the name of St. Thérèse, on whose feast I write, and in the name of St. Francis, whose feast comes tomorrow. It is always a feast where love is, and where love is, God is.

*November 1957*[112]

## Everyone Is Child and Lover

This blindness of love, this folly of love — this seeing Christ in others, everywhere, and not seeing the ugly, the obvious, the dirty, the sinful — this means we do not see the faults of others, only our own. We see only Christ in them. We have eyes only for our beloved, ears for His voice.

This is what caused the saints to go to . . . extremes. . . . The saints rose above the natural, the human, and became supernatural and superhuman in their love. Nothing was difficult to them, all was clear, shining and beautiful on the pathway of love. . . .

What mother ever considers the ugliness of cleaning up after her baby or sick child or husband? . . . To the saints everyone is child and lover. Everyone is Christ.

*June 1944*[113]

## Martyrs at Prayer

"If Stephen had not prayed," writes St. Augustine, "the Church would never have had St. Paul."

*March 1945*[114]

✠

## The Mystery of Love

Only those who keep always in view man's destiny, confident of God's care, only those who pray daily for increase of faith and hope and charity, can endure. St. Stephen prayed for his murderers, *Lay not this sin to their charge.*

And it was to be expected that Jesus Christ would say — He who came to give His life, to lay it down for His brothers — *Father, forgive them for they know not what they do.*

All through the lives of the saints there is this "laying down of life," not the taking of it, this forgiveness, with no thought of revenge, this overwhelming love that overcomes fear, this loving to folly, the folly of the Cross. What are we looking for, what do we expect in this life?

*If they have persecuted Me, they will also persecute you. Blessed are they who suffer persecution for justice' sake, for theirs is the kingdom of heaven.*

*Take up your cross and follow Me. Fear not, for I have conquered death.*

*In the world you shall have distress, but have confidence. I have overcome the world.*

*If you will serve Me, deny yourself. My yoke is easy and My burden light.*

This is the mystery of the Christian life, the mystery of love. Even if we don't understand it, we can pray to understand it, we can pray to grow in love.

*January 1957*[115]

✠

## Saint of 'The Little Way'

All the suffering, the misery of the needy and the groaning of the poor, is part of the world suffering which makes up the sufferings of Christ.

Most of us try to forget and get what joy we can: "eat, drink and be merry." Even the great St. Teresa was said to have remarked as she danced during a recreation hour, to the scandal of the other nuns, "One has got to do something to make life bearable," and the philosophers become existentialist and nurse their noble despair.

One of the reasons I am writing a life of the Little Flower is because she was determined to do something about it, even though she was imprisoned, to all intents and purposes, in a small French convent in Normandy, unknown to all the world. She is the saint of the little way, the saint of the responsible.

She was a saint, so her words were scattered like seeds profligately all over the world. Books about her are read, her autobiography has gone into many editions, but the social implications of her teachings are yet to be written.

The significance of our smallest acts! The significance of the little things we leave undone! The protests we do not make, the stands we do not take, we who are living in the world!

I'm not trying to say that the Little Flower would have gone out on picket lines and spoken on communist platforms or embraced her Protestant neighbors, if there were any in the town of Alençon.

She was a product of her environment, bourgeois, middle class, the daughter of skilled workers, comfortable, frugal people who lived apart from the world with their eyes on God, and yet were very much a part of the world at that time, with the Franco-Prussian war, its aftermath of fear and hysteria and visions and prophecies.

She wanted everything, every apostolate, she said, both when she was a child and later as a young woman, and she used the means at her disposal to participate in everything, to increase the sum total of the love of God in the world by every minute act, every suffering, every movement of her body and soul, done for the love of God and the love of souls. She used the spiritual weapons everyone of us have at our disposal.

*April 1952*[116]

## In the Name of Christ

It is right never to be satisfied with the little we can do, but we must remember the "little way" of St. Thérèse. We must remember the importance of giving even a drink of cold water in the name of Christ.

*March 1938*[117]

## Work As at Nazareth

When a mother, a housewife, asks what she can do, one can only point to the way of St. Thérèse, that *little way,* so much misunderstood and so much despised. She did all for the love of God, even to putting up with the irritation in herself caused by the proximity of a nervous nun.

She began with working for peace in her own heart, and willing to love where love was difficult, and so she grew in love, and increased the sum total of love in the world, not to speak of peace. Newman wrote: "Let us but raise the level of religion in our hearts, and it will rise in the world. He who attempts to set up God's kingdom in his heart, furthers it in the world. . . ."

It is working from the ground up, from the poverty of the stable, in work as at Nazareth, and also in going from town to town, as in the public life of Jesus two thousand years ago. And since a thousand years are as one day, and Christianity is but two days old, let us take heart and start now.

*December 1965*[118]

✠

---

## Their Flesh Is a Battleground

The Little Flower said: "I should not be happy in heaven if I was not able to provide little pleasures on earth for those I love. . . . I shall spend my heaven doing good upon earth." I like these quotations.

Either the Little Flower is looked upon (perhaps because of her nickname) with sentimentality, or, as one gets to know her better, with dread. On that frail battleground of her flesh was fought the wars of today. When she died, her bones were piercing her body and she died in an agony of both flesh and spirit.

She was tempted against faith and said that for the last years of her life she forced herself to believe with her indomitable will while a mocking voice cried in her ears

that there was neither heaven nor hell, and she was fling-
ing away her life for nothing. To her God was a consum-
ing flame.

"*It is a terrible thing to fall into the hands of the living
God,*" St. Peter said with exultation. We have to pay a great
and terrible price but *underneath are the everlasting arms*.
Thank God for the saints whose feast days come around
and remind us that we too are called to be saints.

*October 1949*[119]

✠

## For Our Imitation

It is the feast of St. Patrick today and in the new Maryknoll
missal he is listed as a "pigherd" when he first lived in
Ireland. . . . St. Patrick, the pigherd, the saint and the
scholar; St. Joseph, the carpenter and the saint; St.
Benedict ("work and pray") and St. Isidore, the farm la-
borer, member of the world proletariat — their feasts are
all this week.

They were followers of Christ and the Church raises
them to the rank of canonized saint for our imitation.
We are *called to be saints*, St. Paul said, and Peter Maurin
called on us to make that kind of society where it was
easier for men to be saints. Nothing less will work. Nothing less is powerful enough to combat war and the all-
encroaching State.

To be a saint is to be a lover, ready to leave all, to give
all. Dostoyevsky said that love in practice was a harsh
and dreadful thing compared to love in dreams, but if
"we see only Jesus" in all who come to us — the lame,
the halt and the blind who come to help and to ask for
help — then it is easier. Father Faber says we are pro-

gressing if we begin over again each day in these resolutions.

*April 1958*[120]

## Abandoned to the Will of God

Our Lady gives us the most perfect example of abandonment to the will of God. When Our Lord told us how to pray, and He spoke as one sharing our humanity, He directed us to say, *Thy will be done.*

But it was before His teaching that the Mother He gave us said: *Be it done unto me according to Thy word. . . .* So we say that never could we forget those words of Christ on the Cross — *Behold thy mother.* And we feel her care of us and we are mindful of the great lesson of the Gospel.

*March 1935*[121]

## Prayer to Mary

Dear Mary. . . .
It is easy to give thanks to you, Blessed Mother,
    for all the graces we have received at your hands this
        past year
    and the many years before. . . .
We are asking your prayers, sweet Mary,
    first of all for those who love you so much,
    and we're thinking right now of a man
    brought back to the faith through love for you,
    who speaks with love and admiration and awe
    and all tenderness of "that little Jewish girl, Mary."
He's a dishwasher and a kitchen helper in a big school,
    Mary,

and where he is, you are also,
so bless those students there too,
and all young people
whose hearts burn to serve and carry your banner.
We ask your prayers for the oppressed throughout the
     world —
     for the worker whose mother you are,
     and for the workers who disclaim you as their
          mother,
     and we know that you will remember them all,
     atheist, communist, socialist, as well as
     Catholic and non-Catholic . . .
     for you *are* the mother of them all,
     and your heart must yearn over those children
     who turn from you and forget.
You are the mother of us all —
     Jesus Christ Our Lord gave us all to you
     when He gave himself to death on the Cross
     for love of each one of us.

*May 1937*[122]

✠

---

## Quiet, Strong, and Brave

St. Joseph, patron of the working man, pray for us. We
like to meditate on his acceptance of the role in life as-
signed to him and of his grand and sublime indifference
to created goods.

He was poor, he had only his two hands to provide
food and shelter for his charges. When he was homeless
it was not reported that he grieved, and when he was
forced to flee into Egypt by night he took it not only for

himself, but for his sacred charges. A man, quiet, strong, brave, who never failed in his trust.

*March 1935*[123]

☩

---

### Prayer to St. Joseph

Dear St. Joseph, this is your month . . .
    and a number of our Houses of Hospitality
    are named after you, including the first one, ours in
        New York.
So we honor you now by coming to you with requests,
    showing our faith, our trust in your ever ready help
        and protection.
Help us to keep going so that we can continue to pro-
        test war,
    the blockade, the bombardment of
    cities and civilians. . . .
Please take care of us against all dangers,
    as you protected Mary and Our Lord Jesus Christ
    on the flight into Egypt.
Supply us with our needs,
    you are our householder, the head of our family.
Help us to pay our bills, by reminding our friends of
        our needs.
Today we spent every cent we had — there is nothing
        left but debts. . . .
We would like to be saints,
    we would like to do you honor
    by being as much like you as possible.
But our achievements fall far short of our aspirations.
Hold us up, please, St. Joseph.
And we thank God we have you,

as the Blessed Mother must have thanked God for you every day of her life.

*March 1942*[124]

✠

---

## To Be 'New Men'

November is the month when we should most especially remember the dead. November first commemorates *All Saints*, canonized or uncanonized, and there are undoubtedly more of the latter than the former since, as St. Paul says, we are all *called to be saints*, that is, to be holy, that is, to be whole men, in whom the life of the Spirit has progressively become stronger so that in putting off the "*old man*," we become "*new men.*"

There is a great deal of talk in both Russian and Chinese communist circles about the necessity of becoming "new men," and I hope and pray that Catholics will recognize this necessity too. Christ took on our humanity so that we would put on His divinity. He showed us the way and we are a lifetime learning it.

*October-November 1966*[125]

✠

---

## Give It Up for Him

Yes, Christ did say, *If thou wouldst be perfect.* . . . And we take His command literally. And nobody ever will be perfect while they are enwrapped by possessions. We have to lose even our life before we can find it.

We have to give up all to God. When we die we are "going to carry in our clutched hands only what we have given away." Here or hereafter we are going to have to

126

strip from ourselves (we can do it here of our own will, but it will be done for us in purgatory — that's why it is more generous to do it here) every possession of mind and body and give them up to the Lord.

*January 1936*[126]

✠

## Put Off the Old You

Charles Péguy wrote: "I am afraid to go to heaven alone. God will say to me, 'Where are the others?' " In one sense we live and die alone in an awful solitude. But, joyful thought: we are all members of the same body and our head is Jesus Christ. . . .

Here, too, is the idea of the communion of saints. *When the health of one member suffers, the health of the whole body is lowered.* And contrariwise, if one is uplifted, he lifts others with him. We share in the honor and glory and beauty and love of others. We can draw upon their merits. We are inspired by their example. We are followers of Christ, our head.

St. Paul said to put off the old man and put on Christ. . . . If we embrace poverty we put on Christ. If we put off the world, if we put the world out of our hearts, there is room for Christ within. . . .

To put off the old man means putting off useless reading, much of our newspaper reading, books, movies. This is mortifying the eyes. Making them dead to the world so we can see the true light which is Christ. . . .

The ears. Idle talk. The radio. The world comes into the ears. Suspicion, rancor, hatred, fear, come in through the ears. Perhaps I can learn to control my tongue, practice silence, if I control my ears. . . .

Touch. The pleasures and pains of sense are confused. . . . Christ offered His death for the sins of the world. So we offer our voluntary and involuntary pains and sufferings for the sins of the world, my own and others. Accepting gladly, joyously, no matter how inflicted. To pray with outstretched arms, to keep vigil when the whole body is tortured with the desire for sleep, to scourge oneself to fast.

A German woman doctor who spent a year in a concentration camp for refusing to sterilize epileptics, said that one form of torture inflicted was to turn blinding light into the cells so that the women could not sleep. This is to be keeping vigil with Christ. To keep vigil voluntarily is to be sharing this pain of the world, this agony of the Mystical Body. Insomnia may be keeping vigil.

*January 1944*[127]

✠

## To Train for Love

To train oneself for the race, to train oneself to a joyful acceptance, a loving acceptance. To love one's enemies. *Father, forgive them for they know not what they do.* Jesus said to a fellow-sufferer who accepted his pains, *This day shalt thou be with Me in Paradise.*

St. Peter said, not long after the death of Jesus, *And now brothers, comrades, I know that you acted in ignorance, so did also your rulers. Repent then and be converted.*

What hope! What optimism! What foolishness. It is the folly of the Cross. Can a Hitler be converted and live? *God, I believe, help Thou mine unbelief.* Let me see Christ in him. *Take away my heart of stone, and give me a heart of flesh.* Teach me to love.

Help me, Jesus of Nazareth, King of the Jews, have mercy on me a sinner. Help me to make a tiny beginning by building up the grace and mighty force of love which will overcome fear. How mighty is that force. How terrible and beautiful a thing it is to fall into the hands of a living God. Teach us, God, Holy and Mighty One, what love is!

*January 1944*[128]

✠

### All Things Are Possible to Us

We know that we fail in our love and self sacrifice seventy times seven times daily, but that we must keep on picking ourselves up and going on, and we rejoice in the fact that if we do not strip ourselves for love of brother and of God, God himself will do it for us.

Let us pray He does it gently, little by little, as He comes to us so gently in the Blessed Sacrament each day.

I am sure He will always temper the wind to the shorn lamb, but that does not minimize our realization that we are but dust, and that in following Him we are carrying a cross and are in one way or another going to die on it, that we lose hair, teeth, eyes, hearing, strength — all little by little, and we pray that this purification of the outer man will be matched by an inner purification.

But enough of humility right now. Self esteem tells us that we are sons of God. A triumphant thought. One night many years ago in a lonely moment, in a little town in Arkansas, I woke up with a terrible sense of futility and helplessness.

I thought, "What am I doing traveling around speaking? Who am I anyway to be so presumptuous?" And suddenly a most wonderful sense of the glory of being a child of God swept over me, so joyous a sense of my own importance that I have often reflected on it since.

I would pray that our readers have it, and grow in it, this sense of their importance as temples of the Holy Ghost, sons of God, divinized by His coming. All things are possible to us, we can do all things in Him who strengthens us.

We may look at the George Washington Bridge, great dams in the process of construction, airports, men flying, smashing atoms, deeply plunging into this material world to discover the secrets of the material universe and we may return refreshed to the Gospel which is the tiny mustard seed growing into a great tree throughout the world.

We return, I say, to the work we are doing, the works of mercy, the love of the poor and destitute, the living with others, the writing ideas down on paper and speaking them from platforms, and know that this tiny work, God-given in that we have a vocation . . . is of the greatest and most tremendous importance.

*January 1954*[129]

⁜

## We Have to Begin to See

We have to begin to see what Christianity really is, that *our God is a living fire; though He slay me yet will I trust Him.* We have to think in terms of the Beatitudes and the Sermon on the Mount and have this readiness to suffer.

*We have not yet resisted unto blood.* We have not yet loved our neighbor with the kind of love that is a precept to the extent of laying down our life for him. And our life very often means our money, money that we have sweated for; it means our bread, our daily living, our rent, our clothes. We haven't shown ourselves ready to lay down our life. This is a new precept, it is a new way, it is the new man we are supposed to become.

I always comfort myself by saying that Christianity is only two days old (a thousand years are as one day in the sight of God) and so it is only a couple of days that are past and now it is about time we began to take these things literally, to begin tomorrow morning and say, *now I have begun. . . .*

*April 1968*[130]

✠
_____

## Joy of the Doomed

What is there to expect except suffering in work of this kind? St. Paul said, *Rejoice in tribulation. . . .* The youths of Uganda, Protestant and Catholic, who were buried alive in the 1880s also went to their doom singing hymns. . . .

It is hard to believe and we cringe in fear at the very thought. And we don't believe that we'll ever have the strength to take the way of nonviolence which may result in physical martyrdom.

We don't believe in God's mercy, and we can only say: *Help Thou mine unbelief. . . . Take away my heart of stone and give me a heart of flesh. . . . In Thee have I hoped, let me never be confounded.* These are the acts of faith, hope and charity. . . .

This is the way. This is what converts expect when they come into the Church and they find it in the lives of the saints who accept the idea of death in whatever form it takes. We say all these things in our prayers and don't mean them. And God takes us at our word, fortunately, and so we are saved in spite of ourselves; we are just dragged in by the hair of the head.

God certainly comes to the rescue over and over again and enables us to do what seems utterly impossible. Many a person comes into the Church under utterly impossible circumstances; it as though they were taking their own life, as though they were dying, in order to do this. I have seen people unhinged by it.

We have quite a few with us who are disturbed, who have suffered extremely, have cut themselves off from their families and backgrounds. It is a terrible thing to fall into the hands of the living God. It is not anything that we can take except with the utmost seriousness and yet it is of course the greatest joy in the world.

*April 1968*[131]

## Taken by the Hair

I often feel that if you truly want to do the will of God He will see to it that you do it, even if He has to take you by the hair of your head like Habakkuk and put you where He wants you.

*August 1959*[132]

## A Love to Die For

There is a character in *The Plague*, by Albert Camus, who says that he is tired of hearing about men dying for an idea. He would like to hear about a man dying for love for a change. He goes on to say that men have forgotten how to love, that all they seem to be thinking of these days is learning how to kill. Man, he says, seems to have lost the capacity for love.

What is God but Love? What is a religion without love? We read of the saints dying for love and we wonder what they mean. There was a silly verse I used to hear long ago, "Men have died and worms have eaten them but not for love." I have no idea where it comes from. And nowadays in this time of war and preparing for war, we would agree, except for the saints. Yes, they have died for love of God.

But Camus' character would say, "I mean for love of man." Our Lord did that, but most people no longer believe in Him. It is hard to talk to people about God if they do not believe in Him. So one can talk and write of love. People want to believe in that even when they are all but convinced that it is an illusion. (It would be better still to love, rather than to write about it. It would be more convincing.). . . .

Pascal said of love, "You would not seek me if you had not already found me." . . . Faith is there at any rate. A faith in love, a seeking for love. It is something then to build on, amongst the mass of people who have lost God, who do not know in what they believe though they believe and seek for love.

And where are the teachers to teach of this love, of the stages of this love, the purgations of this love, the sufferings entailed by this love, the stages through which natural love must pass to reach the supernatural?

We would all like to hear of men laying down their lives for love for their fellows, and . . . the Beatitudes and the commandment to love our enemy, do good to them that persecute us. *A new commandment I give you, that you love one another as I have loved you.* One said that who did lay down His life for all men.

*September 1948*[133]

## We Are Not Christians

To be honest we certainly cannot say we are Christians. Being and becoming are two different things. We might better say that unlike the just man who falls seven times daily, we are failing seventy times seven times, to follow in the footsteps of Christ.

*June 1970*[134]

## Ask Her

Without her consent, we would not have Our Lord. She gave Him flesh and blood; it is through her that we have Christ in His humanity. It is said that Christ is present in His humanity . . . in heaven and in the Blessed Sacrament.

And if Christ is there, in His humanity and His divinity, then Mary is, too, with us so close, so eager to dispense His graces. We ask her for the grace we each one stand most in need of, and Our Lord who can deny her nothing will give her more than she asks. And what could she ask more than that her Son be loved, that we may honor Him with increased honor?

*May 1937*[135]

✠

## Ponder These Things

Mary, teach us to pray,
*Be it done unto me according to Thy word.*
Teach us to be silent and ponder these things in our
     hearts, as you did.
Teach us, and comfort us, and care for us as you did
     for Jesus.
And when we are dull and hard of heart, say to your
     Son,
"They have no wine,"
so that we may be strengthened physically as well as
     spiritually,
with the Communion of the Eucharist and
with our sitting down to eat with our brothers.

*May 1954*[136]

# Resources

✠

*There are dozens of good books and other resources on Dorothy Day and the Catholic Worker Movement. The following is a short list of the ones I recommend.*

*Dorothy Day: Selected Writings,* ed. Robert Ellsberg (Orbis). The definitive collection, smartly and sensitively selected and arranged by one of Dorothy's best editors.

*Weapons of the Spirit: Selected Writings of Father John Hugo* (Our Sunday Visitor), ed. David Scott and Mike Aquilina. Dorothy was reading fading typescripts of Father Hugo's writings on her deathbed. She called him "the priest who has influenced my thinking, my understanding of the spiritual life, more than any other."

*The Dorothy Day Library* (http://www.catholicworker.org/ dorothyday/index.cfm) A truly remarkable service to the Church and the world. A growing, searchable on-line database that aims to bring together and make available on the web all of Dorothy Day's writings. The site includes a wealth of other materials related to Dorothy and the Catholic Worker, including information about her sainthood cause.

*Dorothy Day: A Biography,* by William D. Miller. A great book. Astoundingly, it has been out of print for years.

*Love is the Measure: A Biography of Dorothy Day,* by Jim Forest (Orbis). An excellent, short study.

*On Pilgrimage,* by Dorothy Day (Eerdmans). Dorothy's journals from 1948. A beautiful collection of meditations. The book's introduction, by Mark and Louise Zwick, is one of the best introductions to her life and work.

*The Dorothy Day Book,* ed. Margaret Quigley and Michael Garvey (Templegate). A fascinating collection of quotations culled from Dorothy's writings. Shows the wide range of her reading and interests.

*Searching For Christ: The Spirituality of Dorothy Day,* by Brigid O'Shea Merriman (Notre Dame). A very thorough study.

*The Catholic Worker* (36 E. First St., New York, NY 10003). The newspaper started by Dorothy Day and Peter Maurin in 1933, still published monthly, still required reading.

*The Houston Catholic Worker* (P.O. Box 70113, Houston, TX 77270). Probably the best of the Catholic Worker newspapers today. The paper's website (www.cjd.org) has a wealth of background materials on the influences and inspirations for Dorothy's spirituality and social teachings.

# Chapter Notes

✠

## Practicing the Presence of God

1. "Meditation on the Love of God," *Catholic Worker* (April 1935).

2. "The Opium of the People," *Catholic Worker* (July 1937).

3. "A Long Editorial — But it Could Be Longer," *Catholic Worker* (February 1935).

4. "Poverty is the Face of Christ," *Catholic Worker* (December 1952).

5. "Wealth, the Humanity of Christ, Class War," *Catholic Worker* (June 1935). "The Wobblies" is the nickname for the radical trade union, the Industrial Workers of the World, also known as the I.W.W.

6. "Day After Day," *Catholic Worker* (April 1943).

7. "About Cuba," *Catholic Worker* (July-August 1961). Msgr. Romano Guardini (1885-1968) was an Italian-German theologian influential in the liturgical renewal movement leading up to the Second Vatican Council (1963-1965).

8. "Fall Appeal," *Catholic Worker* (October 1964).

9. "On Pilgrimage," *Catholic Worker* (August 1959).

10. "On Pilgrimage," *Catholic Worker* (February 1953). Brother Lawrence (1611-1691) was a cook in a Carmelite convent in France and renowned spiritual adviser. In 1974 Dorothy wrote an introduction to his classic work, *The Practice of the Presence of God,* a collection of meditations.

11. "Aims and Purposes," *Catholic Worker* (February 1940).

12. "Jesus Saith to Them, Come and Dine," *Catholic Worker* (April 1937).

13. "Our Fall Appeal," *Catholic Worker* (October 1946).

14. "Fall Appeal," *Catholic Worker* (November 1957). Mahatma Gandhi, the Indian independence leader, was profoundly moved by his reading of *Unto This Last,* essays on political economy written by the British critic John Ruskin (d. 1900). J. D. Salinger's two stories on the Jesus Prayer were collected in *Franny and Zooey* (1961).

15. "Room For Christ," *Catholic Worker* (December 1945). *Alter Christus* is Latin for "another Christ."

16. "What Does Ammon Mean," *Catholic Worker* (June 1965). The two Teresas are St. Teresa of Ávila and St. Thérèse of Lisieux.

17. "May Day," *Catholic Worker* (May 1954).

## The Way of Love

18. "Notes By the Way," *Catholic Worker* (January 1944). Georges Bernanos, twentieth-century French novelist and essayist, best known for his *The Diary of a Country Priest*. Bede Frost, twentieth-century English Benedictine spiritual writer. Father John Hugo (d. 1985), a Pittsburgh diocesan priest who was Dorothy Day's unofficial spiritual adviser for more than forty years. Fyodor Dostoyevsky, nineteenth-century Russian novelist. *Diligo.* Day was struck by the fact that the Latin verb for love (*diligo*) means to choose or prefer above all else.

19. "Love is the Common Ground," *Catholic Worker* (June 1951).

20. "On Pilgrimage," *Catholic Worker* (April 1948).

21. "Christmas 1949: A Plea for Hospitality," *Catholic Worker* (December 1949). Julian of Norwich (1342-1416), an English mystic, was one of Dorothy's favorite spiritual writers.

22. "On Pilgrimage," *Catholic Worker* (July-August 1950).

23. "Day After Day," *Catholic Worker* (December 1942).

24. "Meditation on the Love of God," *Catholic Worker* (April 1935).

25. "Meditation on the Love of God," *Catholic Worker* (April 1935).

26. "On Pilgrimage," *Catholic Worker* (April 1949).

27. "On Pilgrimage," *Catholic Worker* (April 1948).

28. "Love is the Measure," *Catholic Worker* (June 1946).

29. "What Does Ammon Mean," *Catholic Worker* (June 1965).

30. "On Pilgrimage," *Catholic Worker* (January 1969).

31. "Hell is Not to Love Anymore," *Catholic Worker* (May 1939). *The Brothers Karamazov,* the 1880 novel by Fyodor Dostoyevsky.

32. "What Do the Simple Folk Do," *Catholic Worker* (May 1978).

33. "Love is the Common Ground," *Catholic Worker* (June 1951).

34. "On Pilgrimage," *Catholic Worker* (March 1952).

35. "To Die For Love," *Catholic Worker* (September 1948).

36. "To Die For Love," *Catholic Worker* (September 1948). Father Pacifique Roy, a Josephite priest and retreat leader, who was very close to Dorothy through the 1940s. Gaspé is in eastern Quebec.

37. "The Message of Love," *Catholic Worker* (December 1950).

38. "We Go On Record: CW Refuses Tax Exemption," *Catholic Worker* (May 1972).

39. "The Month of May," *Catholic Worker* (May 1950). The quotes are not attributed in the original.

## Weapons of the Spirit

40. "On Pilgrimage," *Catholic Worker* (July-August 1972).

41. "Christmas," *Catholic Worker* (December 1934).

42. "We Appeal to You in the Name of St. Joseph," *Catholic Worker* (April 1953). *The Way of a Pilgrim* is a nineteenth-century spiritual classic about a Russian peasant's efforts to learn how to "pray without ceasing."

43. "On Pilgrimage," *Catholic Worker* (March-April 1975).

44. "On Pilgrimage," *Catholic Worker* (July-August 1973).

45. "On Pilgrimage," *Catholic Worker* (September 1975). Pope John XXIII (1958-1963).

46. "On Simple Prayer," *Catholic Worker* (March-April 1976).

47. "Day After Day," *Catholic Worker* (November 1936).

48. "Liturgy and Sociology," *Catholic Worker* (January 1936). Prime and Compline are the names, respectively, for the morning and evening prayers of the Church.

49. "For These Dear Dead," *Catholic Worker* (November 1946).

50. "On Pilgrimage," *Catholic Worker* (May 1954).

51. "On Pilgrimage," *Catholic Worker* (June 1967).

52. "On Pilgrimage," (June 1973). The "Jesus Prayer" involves the constant silent repetition of the words "Lord Jesus Christ, Son of God, have mercy on me, a sinner." It is an ancient devotion especially in the Christian East, which Dorothy was particularly fond of.

53. "On Pilgrimage," *Catholic Worker* (October 1955).

54. "Visitation," *Catholic Worker* (July-August 1954). Sister M. Madeleva Wolff, C.S.C., was a poet and a scholar and president of St. Mary's College in South Bend, Indiana.

55. "On Pilgrimage," *Catholic Worker* (September 1974).

56. "Fall Appeal," *Catholic Worker* (October-November 1973). Ducat, a gold coin.

57. "Poverty Incorporated," *Catholic Worker* (May 1950).

58. "We Appeal To You," *Catholic Worker* (October 1951).

59. "On Pilgrimage," *Catholic Worker* (July-August 1973).

60. "On Pilgrimage," *Catholic Worker* (October-November 1972).

61. "On Pilgrimage," *Catholic Worker* (January 1963).

62. "On Pilgrimage," *Catholic Worker* (June 1974).

63. "On Pilgrimage," *Catholic Worker* (September 1977). Chaim Potok (b. 1929), American rabbi and novelist whose work focused on the life of Orthodox Jews.

64. "On Pilgrimage," *Catholic Worker* (December 1955).

65. "Poverty is the Pearl of Great Price," *Catholic Worker* (July-August 1953).

66. "On Pilgrimage," *Catholic Worker* (June 1972).

67. "Notes By the Way," *Catholic Worker* (March 1945). Alphonsus Rodriguez (d. 1617), a contemplative Jesuit.

68. "On Pilgrimage," *Catholic Worker* (July-August 1973).

69. "On Simple Prayer," *Catholic Worker* (March-April 1976).

70. "Day After Day," *Catholic Worker* (March 1939).

71. "On Pilgrimage — Mexican Pilgrimage," *Catholic Worker* (February 1958).

72. "On Pilgrimage," *Catholic Worker* (December 1972).

73. "The Fifth Anniversary of Peter Maurin's Death," *Catholic Worker* (June 1954).

74. "On Pilgrimage," *Catholic Worker* (June 1946). Council of Sens, which was held in France in 1140.

75. "To Die For Love," *Catholic Worker* (September 1948). Hugh of St. Victor, twelfth-century French theologian, philosopher, and mystic.

76. "On Pilgrimage," *Catholic Worker* (December 1975).

77. "On Pilgrimage," *Catholic Worker* (October-November 1972).

78. "On Pilgrimage," *Catholic Worker* (December 1972).

79. "The Council and the Mass," *Catholic Worker* (September 1962).

80. "The Council and the Mass," *Catholic Worker* (September 1962).

81. "On Pilgrimage," *Catholic Worker* (March 1966). A piece inspired in part by a young priest's use of a coffee cup in celebrating Mass at the Catholic Worker. Ven. John Henry Newman was a famous English convert of the late nineteenth century. Father Bouyer was a twentieth-century theologian. Jesuit Father Walter Ciszek spent twenty-three years in a Soviet prison and labor camp in Siberia.

82. "On Pilgrimage," *Catholic Worker* (March 1968). Mary Lou Williams, one of the greatest jazz pianists, was a convert to Catholicism and composed a range of liturgical music. *Kyrie, Sanctus,* and the *Great Amen* are parts of the Mass.

83. "On Pilgrimage," *Catholic Worker* (May 1967).

84. "On Pilgrimage," *Catholic Worker* (January 1962).

85. "Day After Day," *Catholic Worker* (June 1940).

86. "On Pilgrimage," *Catholic Worker* (October-November 1975).

87. "Love is the Common Ground," *Catholic Worker* (June 1951).

88. "On Pilgrimage," *Catholic Worker* (April 1949). Father Pacifique Roy, a Josephite priest, was one of Dorothy's dear friends and, with Father John Hugo, a major influence on her spiritual life. A maniple is a strip of silk worn on the arm of a priest when he says Mass.

89. "Requiem for Father Roy," *Catholic Worker* (November 1954).

90. "Love is the Common Ground," *Catholic Worker* (June 1951).

91. "The Living and the Dead," *Catholic Worker* (November 1956). The *Confiteor* is a prayer of confession and penitence.

92. "On Pilgrimage," *Catholic Worker* (June 1977).

93. "Month of Mary," *Catholic Worker* (May 1940).

## To Be a Saint

94. *Catholic Worker* (September 1933).

95. "Visitation," *Catholic Worker* (July-August 1954).

96. "Review: In Solitary Witness by Gordon Zahn," *Catholic Worker* (June 1965).

97. "On Simple Prayer," *Catholic Worker* (March-April 1976).

98. "On Pilgrimage," *Catholic Worker* (June 1974).

99. "May Day — 1956," *Catholic Worker* (May 1956).

100. "November, Month of Remembrance," *Catholic Worker* (November 1955).

101. "On Pilgrimage," *Catholic Worker* (June 1974).

102. "Have You Ever Been to Jail?" *Catholic Worker* (April 1950). The Curé of Ars is another name for St. John Vianney, the nineteenth-century Frenchman who is the patron saint of parish priests.

103. "On Pilgrimage," *Catholic Worker* (February 1967).

104. "On Pilgrimage," *Catholic Worker* (November 1951).

105. "On Pilgrimage," *Catholic Worker* (September 1949).

106. "Fall Appeal," *Catholic Worker* (October-November 1971).

107. "Poverty and Precarity," *Catholic Worker* (May 1952).

108. "On Pilgrimage," *Catholic Worker* (February 1964).

109. "Notes By the Way," *Catholic Worker* (March 1945).